EVEREST ADVENTURE

The tent was picked up and tossed down the mountain by what seemed like an enormous wind. Stokes was still inside it, tumbling around violently with all his equipment. He was screaming in panic and convinced he was going to die ...

Some other books by C. J. Charley

EXTREME EXPEDITIONS: CONQUERING THE WORLD

Catherine Charley is a writer and teacher who has travelled all over the world. Her experiences include paddling a canoe down a river full of crocodiles and piranha in Peru, white-water rafting in Australia and journeying through north-eastern China in freezing temperatures of −30°C. In between, she worked for Raleigh International and learnt how to parachute and to sail. Catherine is a Fellow of the Royal Geographical Society. She lives in Northern Ireland.

C. J. Charley

EVEREST ADVENTURE

PUFFIN BOOKS

*For Hamish, Nicholas, Robert, Isabel,
Joanna, Charles and Alfred.*

PUFFIN BOOKS

Published by the Penguin Group
Penguin Books Ltd, 80 Strand, London WC2R 0RL, England
Penguin Putnam Inc., 375 Hudson Street, New York, New York 10014, USA
Penguin Books Australia Ltd, 250 Camberwell Road, Camberwell,
Victoria 3124, Australia
Penguin Books Canada Ltd, 10 Alcorn Avenue, Toronto, Ontario, Canada M4V 3B2
Penguin Books India (P) Ltd, 11 Community Centre, Panchsheel Park,
New Delhi – 110 017, India
Penguin Books (NZ) Ltd, Cnr Rosedale and Airborne Roads, Albany,
Auckland, New Zealand
Penguin Books (South Africa) (Pty) Ltd, 24 Sturdee Avenue, Rosebank 2196,
South Africa

Penguin Books Ltd, Registered Offices: 80 Strand, London WC2R 0RL, England

www.penguin.com

First published 2002

1 3 5 7 9 10 8 6 4 2

Text copyright © Catherine Charley, 2002

Set in 11pt Futura Book

Made and printed in England by Clays Ltd, St Ives plc

British Library Cataloguing in Publication Data
A CIP record for this book is available from the British Library

ISBN 0–141–31008–1

Contents

ENTER THE
DEATH ZONE ...

On the morning of 6 June 1924, mountaineers George Mallory and Andrew Irvine left their camp to make for the summit of Everest in their quest to be the first humans to get to the top. A few days later, all hope was given up of ever finding them alive. The two men had simply disappeared without trace.

In 1999 climbers found a body, lying face down in the snow, wearing old-fashioned climbing gear. A shirt tag bore the name 'G. Mallory'.

What drove these two men – and so many others after them – to risk so much for a mountain?

Read on to find out about their incredible stories of bravery and survival in the world's highest place.

CLIMBERS ON THE EVEREST EXPERIENCE

'We stepped up. We were there, the dream had come true ...'
Tenzing Norgay, Sherpa, who reached the summit in May 1953 with New Zealander Sir Edmund Hillary – the first people known to have done so.

'Because it's there.'
British mountaineer George Mallory in answer to the question: 'Why do you want to climb Mount Everest?'

'Regularly, after a few steps, we propped ourselves on our axes and, with mouths wide open, gasping for air, rested thus so that every muscle and fibre could work. Yet I felt I was bursting.'
Italian Reinhold Messner, who, with Austrian Peter Habeler, reached the top of Everest without using bottled oxygen, 1978.

'The wind is really the appalling enemy. It is mind-destroying, physically-destroying, soul-destroying.'
British mountaineer Sir Chris Bonington, 1975.

'I was at the summit for forty minutes, but it felt like five. It was an incredibly emotional experience. I stood there and thought, there is nobody in the world higher than me at this precise moment. It was the best moment of my life.'
British mountaineer Alison Hargreaves, the first woman to conquer Everest alone and without oxygen, 1995.

'Technique and ability alone do not get you to the top; it is the willpower that is the most important. This willpower you cannot buy with money or be given by others ... it rises from your heart.'
Junko Tabei, the first woman to climb Everest, 1975.

'It's an honour to be sitting up here.'
Irish mountaineer Dawson Stelfox, from the summit of Everest, 1993.

THE HIGHEST MOUNTAIN IN THE WORLD

Mount Everest is the highest place in the world. It is an incredible 8,848 m high. The very top of the mountain, the summit, is about 9 km above sea level – that is about the same height as a jumbo jet flies!

Where is it?

Everest lies in a range of mountains called the Himalayas, which is 2,500 km long. There are thirteen other peaks in this range that are over 8,000 m (including K2, the second

highest mountain in the world).

Which continent is it in?
Everest is in Asia. It lies on the border of Tibet and Nepal. The north and east sides are in Tibet and the south side is in Nepal.

Why is it called Everest?
After a British man called Sir George Everest (see page 26).

Does Everest have any other names?
Yes. In Tibet it is called Chomolungma, which means 'Mother Goddess of the World'. The Nepalese name is Sagarmatha, 'Goddess of the Sky'. Local people regard Everest as a holy mountain.

Do many people die on Everest?
Yes. Climbing Everest means taking a huge risk with your life. For every six people who get to its summit, one dies in the attempt.

Why is Everest so dangerous?
It can be very difficult to breathe on the slopes of Everest, especially above 8,000 m. This is because the higher you climb, the harder you must breathe to get oxygen into your lungs. Most people who climb Everest nowadays take bottled oxygen to use for the final part of the climb. This helps, but doesn't solve the problem. There are many other dangers on Everest – terrible weather, sudden avalanches, hidden crevasses, to name but a few.

What is the weather like?
The weather can change rapidly and so it affects climbing conditions and also the timings of expeditions.

Wild winds: The winds are often very strong and may increase very suddenly. Climbers have been blown off the mountain to their deaths. At the peak of Everest climbers can face the hazards of the 'jetstream' – a very strong moving air current in this region which can blow at speeds of more than 400 km per hour.

The monsoon: The best time to try and climb Everest is in the spring (about May), after the winter ends and before the monsoon season begins. Monsoon is the name of a wind that brings heavy rain and very, very bad storms from about June to September.

How cold is it?

It is terribly cold, with temperatures plunging to polar levels. At the top of Everest in May, they range from –5°C in the daytime to –75°C at night. Uncovered flesh freezes very quickly at –75°C, and frostbite can swiftly develop (see page 86). The lack of oxygen also makes people get colder more quickly.

What is the Death Zone?

The Death Zone is the name mountaineers have given to the very top part of Everest, above 7,900 m. It is an incredibly dangerous place as there is so little oxygen available at this height. Climbers cannot stay too long in this area as they will gradually get weaker and weaker. Many people have died here.

AMAZING EVEREST RECORDS

First recorded ascent	Edmund Hillary & Tenzing Norgay, 29 May 1953
First ascent by a woman	Junko Tabei, 16 May 1975
First ascent without bottled oxygen	Reinhold Messner & Peter Habeler, 8 May 1978
First ascent alone	Reinhold Messner, 20 August 1980 (also without bottled oxygen)
Most ascents by one person	10, by Ang Rita Sherpa (all without bottled oxygen) 10, by Appa Sherpa 10, by Babu Chiri Sherpa (see below)
Largest number to reach summit on a single day	40 people, 10 May 1993
Oldest climber to reach summit	Lev Sarkisov, aged 60, 1999
Youngest climber to reach summit	Shambu Tamang, aged 16, 1973
First ascent by a disabled climber	Tom Whittaker, 1998 (lost right foot in a car accident, 19 years earlier)
Fastest ascent	15 hours 56 minutes from Base Camp. By Babu Chiri Sherpa, 2000.
Fastest descent	11 minutes to descend 2,440 m from summit to Western Cwm. By Jean-Marc Boivin, 1988, with a parapente (a light, steerable parachute).

Climbers must be brave enough to cross deep crevasses using ladder bridges.

EVEREST THE MOUNTAIN
Climbing dangers

Everest has many dangerous features to challenge even the most expert climber. Your climb takes you over a tricky combination of ice, snow and rocks. You have to cross ice-fields where the slow-moving glacier may cause enormous towers of ice to topple and crush you at any moment. You have to inch your way over wobbly ladders placed over yawning crevasses and be on a constant look-out for other crevasses opening up beneath your feet. You have to climb up the steep face of the mountain with your life depending on your skill and judgement.

The couloirs (or gullies) on the faces are a natural way for you to make your ascent, but unfortunately they are also a main route for avalanches to make their way down! (You will probably climb these couloirs at night with a head-torch, when the ground is frozen – this makes the conditions a bit safer.) Moving towards the summit itself, you have to make your way along a long narrow ridge with steep drops of thousands of metres on either side. Hopefully, you have a good head for heights!

And remember, because of the lack of oxygen in the air (especially in the Death Zone) even the simplest task, such as clipping yourself on to a rope, can take forever and perhaps seem impossible.

Everest is not an easy climb!

CHOOSING THE ROUTE

Mount Everest can be approached and climbed from several directions. Going up the Kangshung Face on the east side, for example, is incredibly difficult. The skills required mean that only the most expert mountaineers can manage it. Other routes are more straightforward, but they all have their problems.

Everest: important features

Nowadays the most popular way is to climb from the Nepalese side, along the route taken by Hillary and Tenzing in 1953 – the Khumbu Glacier, the Khumbu Ice-fall, the South Col, the South Summit, the Hillary Step, and then on to the summit itself. In theory, a very fit person with some mountaineering experience, a good head for heights, and who is using bottled oxygen, could climb Everest with a guide along this route. However, in practice, it is very dangerous – as the stories in this book show.

Everest is a bit like a pyramid in shape. The mountain has three ridges (a long narrow raised piece of land with sloping sides) and three faces.

THE RIDGES
▲ The North-East Ridge is 5 km in length and runs from the summit down towards Tibet. Early attempts to climb Everest in the 1920s and 1930s were made along this ridge.
▲ The West Ridge is about 5 km long. Some of the most technically difficult climbing on Everest takes place here because of its steep drops and cliffs.
▲ The South-East Ridge is about 1.5 km long and runs into Nepal. This is on the route that Hillary and Tenzing took to the summit in 1953. It is now a popular route for climbers.

THE FACES
4 The South-West Face is a very steep wall of rock and is an extremely dangerous and difficult climb.
5 The North-West Face is concave (dips inwards) and has many couloirs. These provide routes for modern climbers, but there is a high avalanche risk in the lower parts.
6 The East Face (which lies on the other side of the mountain

in this photo) is an enormous area, also known as the Kangshung Face. The East Rib (or 'Fantasy Ridge') is found here. No climber has yet made a full ascent of this difficult ridge.

THE COLS

⑦ The North Col is at the top of several glaciers on the North-East Ridge and is nearly 7,010 m high.

⑧ The South Col is at 7,986 m and leads up to the South-East Ridge and to ☆**The South Summit**.

Everest: Glaciers

Crossing large areas of shifting glacier is part of the Everest experience. On today's main routes the Khumbu Glacier lies on the approach from Nepal while the Rongbuk Glacier stretches across the Tibetan side of the mountain. On the extremely hazardous east approach from Tibet is the Kangshung Glacier.

Tibet and Nepal

At different times both Tibet and Nepal have been closed to foreigners, but now expeditions can climb Everest from either side of the mountain. However, they have to get permission from the country they wish to place their Base Camp in and pay a high fee for a permit (see page 127).

'Growing' Mount Everest

Fifty million years ago the piece of land that is now called India was a very large island. Then it crashed into the continent of Asia. India is still moving north several millimetres a year, pushing the Himalayas upwards as it does so.

GETTING TO
THE TOP

Climbing Everest is not simply a case of hopping off a plane on to the lower slopes and starting to climb. Anyone attempting this challenge needs to be *very* well prepared. There are lots of factors to consider and many things to organize before you go.

Time
Most teams take a year or more to plan their expeditions. When you finally get to the slopes of Everest, you'll need to spend at least four to five weeks getting used to the lack of oxygen (called 'acclimatizing', see page 18) and preparing your camps before you make an attempt on the summit.

Money
Climbing Everest costs a *lot* of money, nowadays more than £20,000 per person! See page 113 for some of the costs.

Support
Most climbers on Everest are taking part in an organized expedition. They usually have other mountaineers climbing and

working with them, as well as people helping with day-to-day living, e.g. cooking and carrying supplies. An expedition doctor is an important member of the team.

Equipment
Lots of special equipment is needed to climb Everest. Everything from climbing boots to tents, from bottled oxygen to ropes must be brought to the mountain.

Food
A climber on Everest needs at least 3,000 to 4,000 calories a day. This is twice a person's normal daily intake. Expedition food has to provide all these calories. It also has to be light to carry and, in practice, it is very difficult to eat as much as you really need to make up for the energy you are burning up. Consequently, you inevitably lose weight!

Setting up camps
Once you get to Everest you have to spend time setting up camps at different levels along your planned route. This usually takes four to five weeks. These camps form a very important part of any expedition because you cannot make the climb in one go. You must make your way up slowly to each camp, gradually getting higher and higher, in order to acclimatize properly (see page 18) before making the final attempt on the summit.

Base Camp
Base Camp is the first and largest camp and the place where most of the organization gets done. On the Nepalese side of the mountain, Base Camp is located on the Khumbu Glacier. All supplies have to be carried here by yaks, mules or porters because there are no roads. On the Tibetan side, the Base

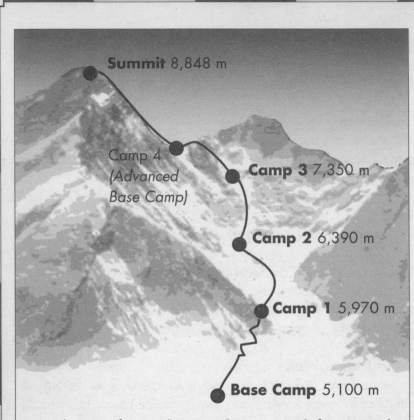

Summit 8,848 m

Camp 4
(Advanced
Base Camp)

Camp 3 7,350 m

Camp 2 6,390 m

Camp 1 5,970 m

Base Camp 5,100 m

Typical camps for South-East Ridge approach from Nepal.

Camp is either in the Kangshung Valley, which is a good trek from the road, or in the Rongbuk Valley, which can be reached over very rough roads.

The equipment for expeditions is brought to and stored at Base Camp while waiting to be carried higher up the mountain. The camp itself is made up of lots of tents – usually several small ones for the team members to sleep in and a larger tent for everyone to eat in, as well as medical and storage tents. Nowadays there is often another tent for communications equipment to link the camp to the climbers on the mountain and also to the outside world.

EXTREME FACTS
HI-TECH EVEREST

These days climbers on their summit attempt often use sophisticated equipment.

Mobile satellite phones and sophisticated radios ('walkie-talkies')	To keep in touch with the rest of your team and to communicate with Base Camp. You can even speak to your family back home as you stand on the summit!
Digital cameras and video cameras	To store and send back fantastically clear images of the mountain, which can be directly viewed via the Internet.
Laptop computers/ expedition web sites	To let the whole world find out about your expedition and keep up with the progress you're making.

We can follow the step-by-step drama of a real expedition with the use of Internet technology. Daredevil adventurer Davo Karnicar (see page 93) took this to the extreme when he decided to attempt skiing down Everest in 2000. A webcam (a video camera linked up to the Internet) was fixed on to his safety helmet, and other cameras were placed on the mountain itself. This meant that people sitting at home could experience the thrill of the world's most challenging ski run for themselves. The event proved so popular that hundreds of thousands of people in more than seventy countries jammed the web site on the day of the run!

Higher camps

Over the weeks before an expedition sets off from Base Camp, the climbers and their support team will set up smaller camps higher up on the mountain, carrying food, equipment and other supplies to them. The routes to the higher camps have to be prepared for people who are carrying heavy loads so that they can ascend in safety.

About two or three camps up from Base Camp is Advanced Base Camp. This is the final camp and the base for the actual attempt on the summit.

GETTING USED TO THE EVEREST AIR

Another important thing to think about up on the slopes of Everest is the difficulty in breathing.

Gasping for breath

If you were transported suddenly from sea-level to the top of Everest, you would die within minutes. This is because your lungs would not be able to get enough oxygen to keep your body going. The higher you climb, the thinner the air is. This means you have to breathe faster and harder (hyperventilate) to get all the oxygen you need. The more used you are to breathing in the air at this incredible height, the better it is for you – but beware, it is *never* easy.

Acclimatization

Anyone attempting to climb Everest has to acclimatize (get used to the altitude) very slowly. This can take anything from thirty to sixty days, depending on the person.

Acclimatization in preparation for the summit day is spread over weeks and usually begins with a few weeks' trek to Base Camp. Then you must make several trips to higher and higher points on the mountain, coming back down to Base Camp again for the night each time. 'Work high, sleep low' is said to be the best way to acclimatize.

You must keep a careful eye on how your body is coping with adapting to the high altitude. If things are going well, you then stay overnight in one of the higher camps before coming down to Base Camp. Gradually, you go up to higher and higher camps for more overnight stays to prepare your body for the summit attempt. However, if you spend much time above 6,000 m you should always go back down to Base Camp to recover – beyond 6,000 m even the most well-acclimatized body will get weaker and weaker.

EXTREME FACTS
ALTITUDE SICKNESS

Altitude sickness is a condition every climber dreads. Caused by the lack of oxygen at high altitudes, every extreme mountaineer will suffer from this sickness to some extent. Expedition members must recognize these signs and know when to stop or to give help to a colleague if the symptoms get really serious:

● Headaches, feeling sick, tired, weak and dizzy.

● Loss of appetite and finding it difficult to sleep.

● Body movements are slow and it takes much longer to perform simple tasks.

● Confused thinking and difficulty in making a decision.

Some people can be so seriously affected by altitude sickness that their brain or lungs stop working efficiently. In very serious cases, the brain will begin to swell up. If this happens it is vital that they go down to a lower point at once or they could die. Even the Base Camps on Everest are too high for some people to cope with.

No one knows how well he or she will cope at these great heights. Even if they have acclimatized well in the past, that is no guarantee that they will do so again. Altitude sickness is very frightening and extremely dangerous. Many climbers have died because of it.

Bottled oxygen

Most climbers aiming for the summit of Everest use bottled oxygen to help them breathe. This is contained in a special cylinder (or bottle) carried on the back and breathed in through a tube linked to a face mask covering the nose and mouth. A climber usually needs three bottles for the final summit attempt. The usual procedure is to set off with two bottles to reach the top and to pick up the third one on the way down from the summit. This will have been left a few days earlier.

Bottled oxygen helps a climber to cope better on Everest, but it does not remove the difficulties caused by the thin air at this height.

Ever since people started to try to reach the summit of Everest, there have been heated discussions about whether this extra oxygen should be used or not. Some think it is cheating to try to get to the top of this natural object with artificial support. The debate still continues among modern climbers. Everest has now been climbed with and without bottled oxygen, but it is certainly much harder without it.

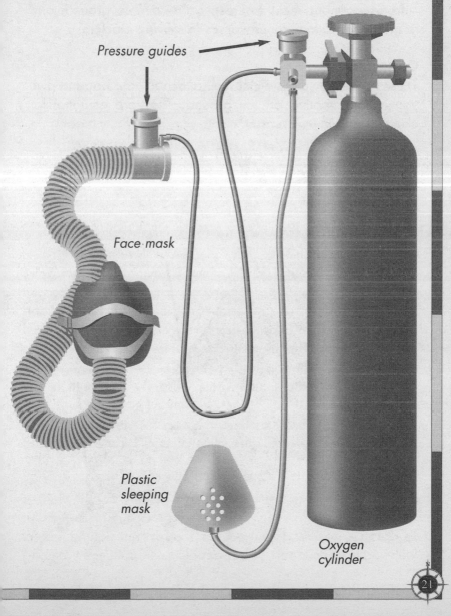

Pressure guides

Face mask

Plastic
sleeping
mask

Oxygen
cylinder

CLIMBING EQUIPMENT AND TECHNIQUES

Mountaineers on Everest need a lot of different types of climbing equipment to help them with the different challenges – from enormous rocks to steep snow-covered ground, and from icy slopes to wide crevasses in moving glaciers.

Crampons

These are metal spikes which you attach to your boots to give you a safer footing on icy ground. They are essential for climbers on snowy Everest.

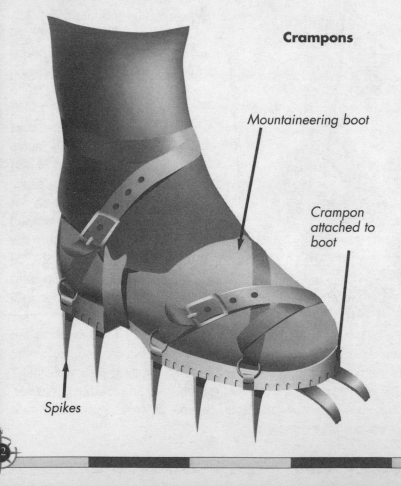

Crampons

Mountaineering boot

Crampon attached to boot

Spikes

Ice-axe

Another very important piece of equipment. The axe can be used for many things:

● As a tool to cut footholds or 'steps' in the ice.

● As a walking stick to keep balance and to support your weight as you make your way up and down the mountain.

● As an anchor in the snow to stop you sliding down the mountain if you slip.

Rope

Nowadays the most steep and dangerous sections on the main routes have ropes fixed along them at the beginning of each climbing season. Climbers clip themselves to these for safety and use them to help pull themselves up. It is often said that the people who do the risky jobs of placing these ropes (or those who climb without them) are the real climbers of Everest.

Pick

Shaft

Spike

Ice-axe

On other routes the lead climber goes ahead and anchors the rope above difficult sections for the other climbers to use. He or she would be attached to a 'belayer', holding another rope for safety.

Climbers also rope themselves together when crossing a glacier, with a long length between each person, in case one of them falls into a covered crevasse.

What to wear for an attempt on Everest

Snowgoggles, to protect eyes from glare

Backpack, will probably include items such as food, drink, radio and extra clothes

Oxygen mask

One-piece hooded windproof suit over a down jacket and pants. Another fibre-filled suit under this layer

Two pairs of fibre and pile mittens worn over silk gloves

Climbing harness

Climbing boots, usually made from plastic to keep feet dry and reduce frostbite risk

Bridging equipment

Glaciers are constantly moving and changing, so every year new ladders and bridges have to be put over the cracks and crevasses on the Khumbu Ice-fall and other parts of Everest. Crawling on one of these ladders over a wide deep drop is very wobbly and scary. There is always the possibility that the crevasse could suddenly widen with the movement of the glacier and you could fall in!

So now you know many of the terrible hazards on the route – read on for tales of extreme adventure, danger and excitement!

FIRST ATTEMPTS

SUNLIGHT LIFT

There is a legend in the Himalayas that the first ascent of Everest was made by a Buddhist saint on a ray of sunlight in the ninth century, when he introduced the Buddhist religion to the people of Tibet.

Since then, reaching the top of Everest has proved much more difficult!

'PEAK XV'

The first sighting by Westerners of the mountain that was to become known as Everest was in the nineteenth century, when teams of British military surveyors journeyed here in order to make reliable maps of the area. On these first maps of the Himalayas, Everest was listed simply as 'Peak XV'. The surveyors calculated it to be the highest mountain in the world and named it after their boss, George Everest, the Surveyor-General of India.

He was unhappy with this and wanted the mountain to have a local name, but it had already become listed as Everest on the maps. In 1865 the Royal Geographical Society (RGS) in London officially adopted the name. Mount Everest it was!

By the 1880s the idea of climbing Everest was being discussed by explorers and mountaineers in the West. A few attempts were made to get closer to the mountain, but it was not until 1921 that members of the RGS and the Alpine Club formed an Everest Committee in London.

Their plan was to send an eight-man team to look for a route up Everest, in preparation for a larger expedition the following year. This team of people included a school teacher called George Mallory who was a very keen and experienced mountaineer. His achievements, adventures and ultimate disappearance on the mountain have meant that his name will always be associated with Everest.

The team explored the possibilities of the northern, western and eastern approaches to Everest. Mallory, together with two other climbers, reached what is now called the North Col by climbing the East Rongbuk Glacier.

FIRST-EVER SUMMIT ATTEMPT

Mallory was also a member of the 1922 expedition, which again approached the mountain from the Tibetan side. In mid-May a group tried for the summit, but it was forced to turn back at 8,170 m after the altitude and exhaustion had got to them.

A narrow escape

As they made their way carefully back down the difficult slopes, one of the exhausted men suddenly slipped and fell. As he did so, he pulled off two of the others who were roped to him. It was terrifying. For a moment it looked as if the whole group of four would plunge to their deaths thousands of metres below. There was only a split second to think – and to act. Instinctively, Mallory, the lead climber, plunged his ice-axe deep into the snow and hurled his whole weight on top of it. With the rope wrapped around both the axe and himself, it was just enough to keep the men from disappearing into the depths below. The group had been lucky this time – Mallory's quick thinking had saved their lives. But sadly it wasn't to be long before a terrible tragedy *did* occur on the slopes.

Disaster

In early June members of the expedition were making a further, and final, attempt on the summit. But as they were high on the slopes, the group was suddenly hit by the might of a terrible avalanche. Its immense weight swept right through them and seven Tibetan porters were killed. The expedition members returned to England with heavy hearts. Everest had claimed its first victims (see pages 83 and 94 for other stories of avalanche crises).

EXTREME FACTS
AVALANCHES

An avalanche is a mass of snow, ice and/or rock sliding down a mountain, destroying everything in its path. Every time snow falls, a fresh layer of it is added to the mountain slope. An avalanche can be caused when these layers of snow and ice become dislodged. Rising temperatures are often the cause of this because the snow is no longer frozen hard. Slopes of 30° to 45° are at the greatest risk.

Sometimes an enormous mass of air is pushed ahead of an avalanche, creating a wind. These blasts can pick climbers up and throw them a vast distance. They can even flatten forests!

Procedures

● If you are unlucky enough to be caught in an avalanche, if at all possible, try to 'swim' on the surface to keep your head above the snow. When the snow in the avalanche stops moving, it solidifies very quickly, becoming as hard as concrete.

● If you are being buried by snow, try to guard your face and create an air pocket around it.

● If you find yourself buried in snow, you will have no idea which way up you are – or in which direction to dig. If you try and dribble, you will know roughly from the direction in which your spit flows (away from the sky) which direction to aim for. Try to move upwards if you possibly can.

However, it is very difficult to dig yourself out of the solid snow of an avalanche. Unless buried people are rescued quickly, they will suffocate to death. If you survive an avalanche, try as quickly as possible to find anyone who is buried and get them out rather than be tempted to go for help. Avalanche victims should be given immediate medical treatment and be warmed up in a sleeping-bag or tent until help arrives.

EVEREST ADVENTURE

VANISHING MEN

INTO THIN AIR

In 1924 one of the biggest-ever mysteries happened in the world of mountaineering. This was the famous disappearance of George Mallory, together with his fellow climber Andrew Irvine, last seen as they slowly made their way towards the summit. And the big question was: did they ever make it to the top? If so, they would have been the first people ever to reach the summit (and not Hillary and Tenzing, who currently have that honour).

It is a mystery that people have been trying to solve ever since.

TO BE THE FIRST

Back in 1924, George Mallory was in his late thirties and was obsessed with the idea of reaching Everest's summit. He felt that, because of his age, it would be the last time he'd have a chance to try. Andrew Irvine was a twenty-two-year-old student.

As with the previous two expeditions, their group approached Everest from the Tibetan side. When they reached the mountain itself, the weather was terrible and delayed their preparations greatly. The bad weather was a great worry to the team, who thought it might be a sign of an early monsoon.

Summit attempt one

It was not until 1 June that the expedition's first summit attempt was made. Mallory and Geoffrey Bruce set off, accompanied by porters but with no bottled oxygen. They set up a camp at 7,710 m on the North Ridge. Unfortunately the winds were incredibly strong all day, continually knocking them off balance. This exhausted them. They decided to retreat. Attempt one was officially over.

Summit attempt two

However, now this camp was fixed for the next summit attempt. The next day Edward Norton and Howard Somervell set off – also without bottled oxygen. The strong wind was still blowing, but they reached the camp at 1 p.m. Norton describes how difficult it was to cope with everyday tasks at this altitude:

'The afternoon was spent as every afternoon must always be spent under these conditions. On arrival one crawls into the tent, so completely exhausted that for perhaps three-quarters of an hour one just lies in a sleeping-bag and rests. Then duty begins to call, one member of the party with groans and pantings and frequent rests crawls out of his bag, out of the tent and a few yards to a neighbouring patch of snow, where he fills two big aluminium pots with snow ...'

The men would return to their sleeping-bags while the snow heated up. Norton then says,

'I can honestly say that I know of nothing – not even the exertion of steep climbing at these heights – which is so utterly exhausting or which calls for more determination than this hateful duty of high altitude cooking.'

Food and Drink on Everest

Eating

Early expeditions in the 1920s relied a lot on local food from Tibet, such as rice, potatoes and eggs – though these often made the team members ill. The teams also brought food from Europe in tins, but these were very heavy to carry up to the higher camps. A more convenient item to carry to these camps was blocks of pemmican (a mixture of dried beef and beef fat to which hot water was added to make a sort of soup).

By the 1950s the Everest expeditions had begun to use powdered and dehydrated food, which was much lighter to carry up the mountain.

These days all kinds of convenient things to eat are available for climbers, from powdered milk and pasta to packet soup and fruit juice mixes.

Drinking

Although climbers on Everest are surrounded by frozen water in the form of snow and ice, the snow must be melted to get a drink. This takes a very long time up at altitude, because fuel for the stoves needs oxygen in order to burn properly. The higher up you are, the longer the heating process takes. And, of course, climbing is very thirsty work, so getting enough to drink is very important.

The following day Norton and Somervell set up their next camp at 8,200 m. This was the highest point anyone had ever reached without bottled oxygen. They had to build a platform of rocks for their tent because there was nowhere on the North Ridge flat enough to put one up. After they had sent the porters back down, they went through the same lengthy process of heating water and making food, resting, exhausted, in between times in their sleeping-bags.

Next morning they got away early, at 6.40 a.m. They hoped that all their efforts would be worth it and that that day would be the day to conquer the summit.

Coughing fits

The men continued climbing very slowly upwards, gasping for breath in the thin air. Somervell was now beginning to feel extremely unwell. He had been suffering – like Mallory and some of the others – from an incredibly sore throat, but now he was also having great difficulty breathing. He kept having terrible coughing fits, which sapped his energy further. The cold dry air on Everest (even at Base Camp) often leads to bad coughs and sore throats.

Somervell knew he had to stop for a while, but he encouraged Norton to continue. So Norton went on alone, making his way up over a difficult slope of rock covered with snow. He later described it as being like tiles on a sloping roof: one slip would have sent him to his death, way below.

Double vision

Norton was also getting very tired and, to make things worse, started suffering from double vision (seeing things in twos). This had probably been caused when he had taken his snow goggles off earlier – they had made it difficult to see his boots when he was climbing the loose rocks. Norton should have worn them all the time because, even away from the snow, the thin mountain air meant the glare of the sun was very bright.

He knew that he should turn back. He had reached 8,573 m.

EXTREME FACTS
THE DANGEROUS SUN

The glare of the sun is particularly fierce when it is reflected off snow and ice. Climbers must try to protect themselves from two nasty conditions.

Snow-blindness

This is sunburn of the eye. It normally occurs on very bright days on snowy mountains when climbers are not wearing sufficient eye protection. It can develop eight to twelve hours after actually being exposed to the bright light. To begin with, the sufferer only feels a little discomfort, but then it gets more painful:

- The eyes start to feel as though they are full of sand. They will become red, watery and sore.
- The eyelids may swell up. In bad cases the sufferer can go blind for several days.

Cold padding placed on the eyes and staying in the dark can ease the pain. Mostly the eyes get better within a few days, but sometimes they are damaged for ever. Eye protection (goggles or sunglasses) should be worn all the time on snow and at high altitude. Even on cloudy days and in snowstorms, there is a danger from the reflection of the ultra-violet light.

Sunburn

This is also common at high altitude, especially when the climber is walking over snowy ground. Sunscreen and lip protector for mountaineers should be at least

SPF (Sun Protection Factor) 25. The lips and the nose are particularly likely to get sunburned. Scarves, hats and face masks help give protection.

On this expedition in 1924, the fair-skinned Irvine suffered terribly from sunburn, especially on his face and lips, which were sore and cracked, making eating and sleeping almost unbearable. In those days the kinds of high-protection sun creams we use now did not exist.

A brush with death

A disappointed Norton rejoined Somervell and the two men began their descent together. Both were exhausted. Suddenly Somervell was overcome by the coughing fit of all coughing fits. Something had stuck in his throat and was stopping him from breathing. He gasped but could not get any air into or out of his lungs. As he fell down into the snow, he couldn't even draw breath to call out to Norton for help. Norton continued on walking, completely unaware that his friend behind him was close to death. Somervell was terrified. He thought that he was going to die here on this mountainside not far from his friend.

As a last resort he pushed on his chest with both hands as hard as he could ... and the blockage in his throat came up. He took a great breath and with relief realized that the danger was over. In fact, his breathing was better than it had been for days. Do you know what had happened? He had coughed out the entire lining of his throat! His terrible coughing fits of the last days had loosened it. Everest can be hard on human health in all sorts of ways.

Safety

Eventually they reached the camp where Mallory and the others gave them much-needed tea and soup. They were very dehydrated and desperate for a drink. In addition Norton went totally blind that night and it was nearly three days before he could see again – a very frightening experience.

EXTREME FACTS
DEHYDRATION

Two-thirds of the human body is made up of water. Dehydration happens when you lose too much of it. This is something extreme climbers have to be very careful about.

● The effect of breathing hard and with great difficulty at high altitude makes you lose about 3 litres of water a day into the air.
● The sheer effort of the climb makes you sweat and lose a lot of water.
● The cold dry air at altitude adds to the drying-out process of the body.

Dehydration can increase the effects of altitude sickness, i.e. headaches, dizziness, weakness, confusion and sleeplessness. Mountaineers, especially those climbing to great heights, must make sure they have a lot of liquid with them to drink – 4 litres a day are recommended.

THE FINAL ATTEMPT

While Norton lay blinded, Mallory asked him if he could make one further attempt for the summit before the monsoon arrived. He wanted to try with oxygen and he wanted Irvine to go with him. Because Norton was expedition leader, Mallory had to get his permission.

Norton supported Mallory but he was surprised by his choice of partner. Irvine had much less climbing experience than other members of the team. However, he had proved that he was very able with the oxygen equipment and had spent a lot of time modifying it by making it lighter and more efficient.

Maybe Mallory felt that Irvine's skill in this area was much more important than his climbing abilities. Together, the two of them had been trying out the oxygen equipment. Despite its bulkiness and weight, it had greatly improved their progress on the mountain. Mallory was determined to take every opportunity to achieve his goal.

The big day

On 6 June Mallory and Irvine set off after a breakfast of fried sardines, hot chocolate, biscuits and tea. They had their oxygen packs strapped to their backs. One of the team members, Dr Noel Odell, took an informal photograph of them as they made their final preparations. No one knew it then, but this would be the last photograph ever taken of them alive. Somervell lent them his collapsible 'flat pack' Kodak Vestpocket camera to take pictures at the summit to prove they had got there.

Eight porters accompanied them with food, fuel, spare oxygen and sleeping-bags. The porters themselves were not using oxygen because the expedition had not brought enough for them. (In fact, only thirty-five of the fifty oxygen cylinders sent from England had contained any oxygen when they arrived at Base Camp!)

Once Mallory and Irvine had put on their oxygen face masks they couldn't speak to each other. They could only indicate ideas and directions to each other with signs and touches. Their heavy oxygen systems hissed and wheezed as they breathed in and out. The face mask dug into the sunburn on Irvine's face and made the pain even worse. He had already written in his diary on 3 June:

'A most unpleasant night when everything on earth seemed to rub against my face, and every time it was touched bits of burnt and dry skin came off, which made me nearly scream with pain.'

But despite his discomfort, he was determined to join Mallory in his summit attempt.

Good progress

The weather over the next two days was good and the climb went well. When the porters arrived back they had a note for Odell from Mallory which read:

'Perfect weather for the job!'

Sending Messages
In the days before radio communications, members of expeditions to Everest would send porters up and down the mountain with handwritten notes.

Going for the summit

Mallory and Irvine's final camp (Camp 6) was made about 600 m below the summit. From here they would have to make their way up over dangerous terrain (see map).

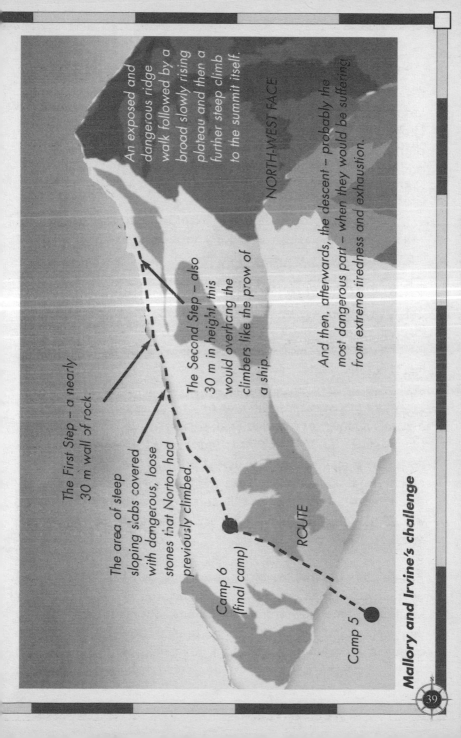

The First Step – a nearly 30 m wall of rock

The area of steep sloping slabs covered with dangerous, loose stones that Norton had previously climbed.

The Second Step – also 30 m in height, this would overhang the climbers like the prow of a ship.

An exposed and dangerous ridge walk followed by a broad slowly rising plateau and then a further steep climb to the summit itself.

NORTH-WEST FACE

And then, afterwards, the descent – probably the most dangerous part – when they would be suffering from extreme tiredness and exhaustion.

Camp 6 (final camp)

ROUTE

Camp 5

Mallory and Irvine's challenge

It would be a very, very tough and long day's work to achieve all this.

Mallory's message had also stated that he and Irvine wanted to start early to make the most of the good weather. Mallory was always keen to get going when he was climbing. Probably, he aimed to start around 6 a.m. But we can only make guesses as to what happened that day because the two men left no written information behind in their tent.

The closest account that we have is from the words and writings of Odell, who was nearer to them than anyone else at the time and had the best experience of that day's conditions.

THE LAST SIGHTING

Odell was climbing up to get the last and highest camp ready for Mallory and Irvine's return when he caught a glimpse through the clouds of two small black specks moving on the ridge above him. He later wrote:

'My eyes became fixed on one tiny black spot silhouetted on a small snow-crest beneath a rock-step in the ridge; the black spot moved. Another black spot became apparent and moved up the snow to join the other on the crest. The first then approached the great rock-step and shortly emerged at the top; the second did likewise. Then the whole fascinating vision vanished, enveloped in cloud once more.'

Odell thought that the black spots must be Mallory and Irvine on their way up the Second Step. But he was worried about their position – some 300 m from the summit. By his reckoning, they only *just* had time to get there and back in daylight. He kept on climbing, wondering what might have delayed them – trouble with the oxygen perhaps? As he reached their last camp, at around 2 p.m., it was beginning to snow and the wind blew more coldly. It appeared that Mallory and Irvine had used oxygen for sleeping because there were used oxygen cylinders inside the tent.

Watching

Odell couldn't stay at this camp to welcome the pair back because there was only room for two people in the tiny tent. That night, from two camps below, Odell watched with John Hazard in the moonlight to see if they could see Mallory and Irvine above as they made their way down. It was a fine clear night, so they were not too worried.

Concerns

But the following day the watchers could still see no sign of movement through their binoculars. They began to get concerned. At midday Odell climbed to the next camp with two porters. He slept little there that night. There was a strong wind and it was very cold, even inside two sleeping-bags and with all his clothes on. What hope was there for Mallory and Irvine in these conditions?

Odell set off again the following morning on his own to the highest camp. He was now worried, very worried. The tent was exactly as he had left it two days before; just a pole had collapsed in the wind. Mallory and Irvine had obviously not been back there.

What now?

Could Mallory and Irvine still be alive? Odell immediately started off in the direction they had probably taken.

It was a lonely, distressing search. Odell found no sign of them and no clue to where they might be or what might have happened. He returned to the tent in a state of despair. Now he had to give the awful news to the rest of the team down below.

Signals

Remember that this was in the days before mountaineers had radios. The team had pre-arranged signals to send news of emergencies down the slopes. Odell dragged the two sleeping-bags out of the tent and laid them out in the shape of a T on a patch of snow. Hazard, watching 1,200 m below, knew that this meant that Mallory and Irvine were nowhere to be seen. They were missing, presumed dead.

Odell closed the tent and set off down the mountain. The wind was now very fierce and very cold. He rested occasionally behind a rock to get away from its wild strength. When he reached Hazard, they dragged six blankets to a snow patch on the edge of the drop and placed them in an X. The message was seen below and understood. It meant, 'No trace can be found, given up hope.'

Odell, Hazard and the last porter set off down the Col sadly to join the others.

GOING HOME

By 13 June everyone had left the mountain and returned to Base Camp. They were very aware of the two empty places at the table.

Norton busied the team with packing to leave for Darjeeling, but his main worry was what to write back to England. On 11 June he had sent a coded message from Base Camp by runner and it reached England eight days later. It read:

**MALLORY IRVINE NOVE REMAINDER ALCEDO,
NORTON RONGBUK.**

Those reading it in London understood it: Mallory and Irvine had died when trying to make a last attempt on Everest's summit. Everyone else was safely at Base Camp.

It was the Royal Geographical Society which had to tell the families of the dead men. They also gave the news to the press, which *The Times* announced on 21 June 1924.

MALLORY AND IRVINE KILLED IN LAST ATTEMPT

The world began to wonder if Mallory and Irvine had managed to get to the top before they disappeared. This is a question that has haunted climbers ever since.

EVEREST ADVENTURE

THE SEARCH FOR MALLORY AND IRVINE

Since 1924 many have tried to solve the mystery surrounding Mallory and Irvine's disappearance. Did they reach the summit?

Many theories have been put forward about their final hours. The clues are like those in a detective story. The key ones are:

1 The last sighting

Odell was the last person to see them. He said they were on the Second Step and 'going strong' for the top. He always felt sure that they could have reached the summit. Because the Second Step was thought to be the last major obstacle before the top, he believed they could have made it. But in later years, as the debate continued, Odell became less sure and he said maybe it was the First Step he had seen them on.

2 The 1924 ice-axe

In 1933 another British expedition attempting to climb Everest

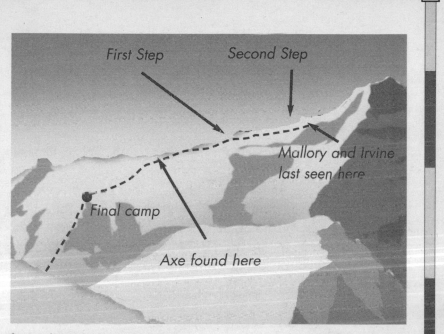

First Step

Second Step

Mallory and Irvine
last seen here

Final camp

Axe found here

from the Tibetan side found an ice-axe. It was about 90 m below the First Step. This find raised a lot of questions. Had this axe belonged to one of the men? Was this the spot where Irvine and Mallory had fallen – perhaps on the way down in the dark? Or had the axe been dropped? Eventually, one of these questions was answered. In the 1960s the axe was identified as Irvine's by his brother.

3 'An English dead'

After the Second World War, the Tibetan approach – Mallory and Irvine's route – to Everest was closed to Westerners. Hillary and Tenzing's successful summit achievement in 1953 (see pages 65–79) was made from the Nepalese side of the mountain. Only Chinese expeditions continued to follow in Mallory and Irvine's footsteps from the Tibetan side.

In 1979 a Chinese climber, Wang Hungbao, reported that on an expedition four years before he had found what he described as 'an English dead'. The body had been seen just a short walk from one of their camps – at about 8,100 m. Wang said that the body had been very old and that the clothes had fallen apart when touched. Wang also said there had been a hole in a cheek where it had been pecked by birds.

The day after he had given this information, Wang himself was killed in an avalanche.

The mystery deepened. This body was near the place where Irvine's ice-axe had been found. Perhaps Wang really had found Irvine's body. Irvine may have fallen and then tried to struggle back to the camp before being defeated by the extreme cold at 8,230 m and lying down to die of exposure.

EXTREME FACTS
EXPOSURE AND HYPOTHERMIA

Exposure is what happens when a person is caught in very bad weather conditions without sufficient protective clothing and the body temperature drops. This can easily happen when a sudden storm whips up on a place like Everest. Hypothermia is when the body temperature drops to dangerously low levels. Early symptoms include feeling cold and numb, having difficulty walking and talking and feeling unenthusiastic about carrying on. The body has already redirected the blood from the arms and legs to keep the central organs of the body warm, such as the heart, brain and lungs. Severe hypothermia happens when shivering stops, the muscles become stiff and unco-ordinated and the person gets confused. Their heartbeat also becomes very weak and slow and it's difficult to tell if they are still breathing.

The treatment is to warm the person slowly with shelter, extra clothes and sleeping-bags. In the Death Zone area of Everest, where helicopter evacuation is impossible, someone affected like this usually has little chance of survival.

4 Other ideas

From 1979 Westerners were again allowed through Tibet to climb Everest. These climbers of the 1980s and 1990s found that the Second Step was not as difficult to climb as it looked from below. They also checked the view Odell would have seen as he looked up at the 'two spots' through the gap in the clouds on that fateful day in 1924.

The First Step could hardly be seen from there, while the view of the Second Step fitted his description. Perhaps Odell's opinion that Mallory and Irvine could have reached the summit was also correct.

But no one knew for sure. The mystery of the vanished men continued to be discussed and all mountaineers on Everest continued to look out for any traces of those two brave early climbers. But for a long time nothing more was found. Would Everest keep its secret for ever?

THE BIG FIND

In 1999 an expedition was put together especially to look for traces of Mallory and Irvine. It was called the Mallory & Irvine Research Expedition and included people from several countries. They had done a lot of research and knew where they wanted to look for key evidence – near the Chinese expedition camp where Wang had found the 'English dead'. They wanted to see if they could find either of the climbers' bodies and, especially, their camera. A photograph of the two men on the summit would prove once and for all that they had been the first people to reach it. Kodak, the camera's manufacturer, felt the pictures could still be processed after being preserved on the deep-freeze conditions of Everest's upper slopes.

On 1 May, the team was ready to begin its task. Five climbers set out to search the high slope. The weather was clear and dry, which helped them feel positive. They fanned out and began their search.

But it was not easy. The area they were searching was about the size of twelve football pitches and at a very steep angle of 30°. Loose stones made it difficult to gain a foothold and this perilous slope led to a great drop on to the Rongbuk Glacier. The searchers had to be very, very careful not to slip off. In addition, even with bottled oxygen, they had to take about three breaths between every step.

The searchers were widely spread out now in among the rough boulders and stones. They kept contact with each other and their Base Camp by radio. American mountaineer Conrad Anker was searching towards the lower edge of the slope. He felt that a body falling from the North-East Ridge (where Irvine's ice-axe had been found) was most likely to be here.

Bodies

And indeed there were several frozen bodies here, but he saw from their modern clothes that they could not have been those of Mallory and Irvine. Anker didn't go too close. He didn't want to disturb them. They had all obviously fallen from the North-East Ridge. Would he find a body from an earlier period here too?

Suddenly something white caught his eye. It looked like a rock but it was much whiter. Anker moved slowly over to investigate. He peered down in disbelief. This too was a body, but it was much older than the others. This one was wearing hobnail boots! He knew it must be Mallory or Irvine because no other climber lost on this side of Everest would have been wearing such old-fashioned boots. Anker could not believe what he was looking at.

A coded message

Anker quickly radioed the others:

`'The last time I tried a boulder in hobnail boots I fell off.'`

A strange message but the others knew the word 'boulder' meant he had found Mallory or Irvine. They had decided to use various code words because everyone nowadays on Everest has radio sets and they can easily listen in to the messages of others. The word 'gorak' (the raven-like bird on Everest) would mean a camera had been found.

The searchers began to move down to Anker.

Moving together

Below at Base Camp, the support members of their expedition watched through a telescope as the five climbers drew together. They knew something was up, but what? The suspense was enormous.

As the search party drew near the body they felt a great sense of awe for this man from nearly eighty years before them who had climbed so high in his old-fashioned boots. The body was white because the sun had bleached it, but there were still pieces of the climber's clothes on it. He had been wearing a canvas-type outer garment, a fur-lined, motorcycle helmet-type hat, a woollen pullover and trousers, a flannel shirt and several layers of cotton and silk underwear.

A broken rope was round his waist. The goraks had eaten into part of the body.

Clinging on

The man was lying face down with his arms stretched out up above his body and his hands were dug deep into the ground. He was clinging on to the mountain. He had been determined to use his last ounce of strength to stop himself from sliding over the drop on to the glacier far below. His right side looked badly battered. His left leg was crossed over his right ankle, perhaps to protect it. He must have been in great pain as he lay there, nevertheless he had hung on.

But was it Mallory or Irvine?

A laundry tag on the shirt read 'G. Mallory'.

In the presence of a hero

But what was to be done now? All climbers have the greatest admiration for Mallory, a veteran of three Everest expeditions in the 1920s. Would it be more respectful to the great man if they did not disturb him in his final resting-place?

After much discussion, everyone agreed that Mallory would probably have wanted them to look for clues about whether he reached the summit. Before they touched him they took photographs of the body as they had found it.

The searchers found a pouch around his neck with personal letters and notes. They also found other items, including goggles, in his pockets. But there was no sign of any camera.

A reburial

Before they left the site they decided to completely cover up Mallory's body to give it dignity in death and to protect it from the goraks. Then they performed a short religious ceremony which an archbishop from the Church of England had given them.

More clues

Over the next few days, the team got two further clues to add to their knowledge of the Mallory and Irvine summit assault:

● A 1924 oxygen cylinder was found just below the First Step.

● One of the group tried to see if he could climb up to the top of the Second Step without using the aluminium ladder the Chinese had placed there in 1975. He nearly did, via a crack – it was dangerous but possible. So Mallory and Irvine could perhaps have managed it.

DID THEY MAKE IT?

Since the finds of the 1999 Mallory & Irvine Research Expedition, there has been a great deal of discussion about whether Mallory and Irvine really did reach the top of Everest before they died.

Arguments *for*

● Mallory's goggles were found in his pocket. This means he probably took them off because it was dark, so it is likely that he was climbing down from the summit when he fell.

● He had no oxygen bottles or any oxygen-carrying apparatus attached to his body, so he had probably used it all up and taken off the heavy equipment. He would have needed all this oxygen for reaching the summit.

● No photo of his wife was found in his possessions. He had always said that he would place this photo on the summit if he reached it.

Arguments *against*

● Mallory could have taken two sets of goggles with him, the ones in his pocket being his spare set. He could have fallen in daylight wearing his other set and had them ripped off as he fell.

● Mallory may have laid the photo of his wife on the highest point that he was able to reach. The weather would have destroyed the photo years ago, so we will never know.

● There are also questions about the Second Step: if they did get up this obstacle, how did they get down again? There is no evidence of an anchor for a rope for them to abseil down.

Unsolved mystery

Mallory and Irvine could have reached the top of Everest in 1924 but we may never know for sure. Other clues may be found at some later date. But whether they reached the top or not, all Everest climbers have a great respect for Mallory and Irvine. They climbed higher than anyone before, on a completely unknown route and without any radio contact with those below – it was an amazing achievement. They were amazing men.

Alpine Club Gong
An oxygen cylinder from the 1924 expedition that was found on Everest in 1933 is now used as a gong in the Alpine Club in London, England.

THE ABOMINABLE SNOWMAN

Huge footprints in the snow, glimpses of a wild and frightening bear-like creature, strange stories told by the local people ... for many years, the legend of the Abominable Snowman has been associated with the Himalayas. But what is this creature, otherwise known as the yeti? Is it a yet unidentified animal or something more sinister?

A new route up

After Mallory and Irvine's disappearance in 1924 the Tibetan government refused all access to Everest until the 1930s, when there were four more official British attempts. All climbed to great heights but still no one reached the summit. After the Second World War Nepal began to allow Western climbers on to the slopes of Everest.

In 1951 a British expedition, led by Eric Shipton, travelled through Nepal to the side of the mountain that had never been climbed or explored by Westerners before. The expedition found a way up through the dangerous ice-walls and crevasses of the Khumbu Ice-fall until they were blocked by an enormous

90 m wide crevasse. But they were excited. They reckoned there was a definite possibility of a route to the summit from this side of the mountain.

They also made another discovery – one that really shook the public's imagination ...

Strange footprints

The expedition brought home photographs of the footprints of a strange creature – at least 30 cm in length (an ice-axe had been placed beside them to show the size). Another

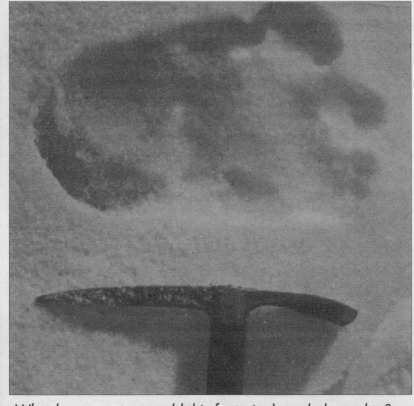

What huge creature could this footprint have belonged to?

photograph showed a line of prints disappearing into the distance.

Did these belong to the Abominable Snowman that was talked about in the folklore of the Himalayan people?

EXTREME FACTS
THE ABOMINABLE SNOWMAN LEGEND

According to legend, the Abominable Snowman (or yeti) is supposed to be half man and half ape and lives in the high snowy areas of the Himalayas where no human has ever ventured. It walks upright on two feet and is taller than a human being. It travels by night and eats the yaks of the poor mountain farmers – it can kill them with a single blow. It moves large rocks in its search for food. There are stories of the Abominable Snowman standing up on its two hind feet and hurling rocks at people if it is disturbed. Some tell of it dragging off young girls to its cave. Others say that to see one means that you will have bad luck. But there are also people who feel that the creature has human-like feelings and a tender side to its character.

Yeti fever

In England *The Times* newspaper covered the story on 6 December 1951 in an article written by Eric Shipton. He said that a Sherpa had confirmed that the footprints were yeti tracks. He described what the footprints looked like:

Where the ice was thin we came upon a well-preserved impression of a creature's foot. It showed three broad 'toes' and a broad 'thumb'.

The experts in England had mixed opinions on the findings. Some thought they were the footprints of a large monkey; others, of a new species that was a cross between a bear and an ape.

However, there were others who thought Shipton was having a practical joke – he was known to enjoy making fun of so-called 'experts'. Some said that the tracks going into the distance seemed, on closer examination, to look like normal goat prints. Shipton, however, always claimed he had told the truth.

FACT OR FICTION?

In the high snowy Himalayas it is difficult to find the truth behind the story of the yeti. But many people have tried. One of these people is Reinhold Messner, a true Everest veteran (see page 88). He was one of the first pair of people to climb Everest without bottled oxygen and he later did it again, this time on his own! Since these achievements he has spent many years climbing in the Himalayas and looking for the Abominable Snowman after a frightening encounter he had with a yeti-like creature in 1986.

Confronting the yeti

Messner was trekking through Tibet, along mountain tracks that no Westerner had ever been near. He was high up, not far from the edge of the tree line. It was getting towards evening and the rays of the sun were too low to reach through the branches. As the sun began going down, the air felt chilly. The forest around him began to look very spooky. Soon it would be too dark to see anything. Messner moved on faster, hoping to find a place where he could settle down safely for the night.

Suddenly something stepped out of the darkening

shadows into a clearing in the forest in front of him. The creature stood still. It was probably about 9 m away, but even at this distance Messner could feel the hairs on the back of his neck stand up with fear.

What was it? He had never seen anything like it before. Then, just as suddenly, the creature moved off again into the forest.

Slowly Messner crept forward to the place where it had been. There on the ground in front of him was an enormous footprint!

He could see the toes. He touched the mud. It was definitely a fresh mark made by the creature he had seen. And the animal must have been pretty heavy. Messner's own boots did not sink into the mud nearly as deeply as the bare foot of this animal.

He took a photograph of the footprint, annoyed with himself that he hadn't taken a picture of the creature itself. But he had been too shocked by the sight of it to react quickly.

A second sighting

Feeling nervous, Messner made his way through the trees until he came to the edge of the forest. Then he moved into the open, pushing his way through some bushes as he did so. The moon was now visible up in the sky above him. Suddenly he heard a weird whistling sound. Just out of the corner of his eye he caught sight of an upright shadow moving along the edge of the trees on two legs.

Whatever it was stopped, stood still and turned to look at him. Messner could see the creature clearly in the strengthening moonlight, its eyes and teeth glistening. It was tall, possibly about 2 m in height, and threatening. It seemed to be covered in black hair. Strong arms hung down almost to its knees and it had short but powerful legs. Again Messner heard the whistling sound, but now it sounded more like an angry hiss.

There was a strange, strong animal scent in the air too – a horrible smell. Messner watched, rooted to the spot, as the creature began to run forward, still upright, making its way out of the forest area into the bushes beyond. The moonlight picked it out clearly against the black of the forest. It stopped again, as if to catch its breath, but it didn't look back this time.

The creature now plunged into the larger bushes in the clearing, Messner could hear it making its way through them. When it came out into the open again it was moving fast up the slope on all fours. Messner watched as it gathered speed and galloped higher up the mountain, eventually disappearing into the night above.

Only then did he realize that his hands were trembling.

Panic

By now Messner was extremely shaken and he knew he didn't want to spend the night out in the open. He kept going until he found a small village. Here he tried to explain to the Tibetan people what he had just seen, using many gestures as he couldn't speak much of their language.

'Chemo!' they whispered to each other, 'Chemo!' They said the word with a mixture of fear and respect.

Was this their name for the yeti? Messner wasn't sure. But in the safety of the village he was at least able to get some sleep that night.

The next morning one of the Tibetans offered to act as a guide for Messner. A few hours later he suddenly stopped and pointed to the ground near some rocks. Again he said the word, 'Chemo!' Again Messner saw huge footprints. He also realized that these large chunky rocks had been recently moved – perhaps to look for food. The guide pointed up the mountain, showing that the chemo lived up there. 'They are like a bear, but also like a man,' he said.

Messner was hooked. Were the yeti and the chemo one and the same, he wondered. Had he really seen a yeti? Could he find one again, take a photograph and prove that this so-called mystical creature existed after all?

Search

Over the next few years Messner set out to find the truth. He trekked around the Himalaya Mountains especially to search for this creature. He had many adventures along the way and caught more glimpses of it. He also met people who had seen chemos. He saw more footprints, but never seemed to be able to catch the animal itself in a photograph.

Thoughts

However, reluctantly, Messner now believes that the yeti is really an unknown species of enormous brown Himalayan bear. He thinks that the footprints he has seen are probably made as the bear stepped with its back feet on to the prints of its front feet. He believes that, because an isolated community might only have one sighting every ten years, the myth continues.

But, says Messner, this type of enormous brown Himalayan bear is a very frightening monster in itself!

Yeti tales

But not everyone is sure about Messner's theories. The myth of the yeti has been around for centuries among the Himalayan people – and the Himalayas are a very big area.

Sherpa Kancha Namche displays the famous yeti scalp, a treasure of the local monks.

Some people still believe that there is an Abominable Snowman, a beast much, much bigger than the brown bear, even now waiting to be scientifically recorded by humans. This could be a creature from an ancient species that has managed to survive undiscovered.

Maybe it sits high up in Himalayan snow caves laughing at our attempts to disprove its existence. Maybe, one day, all the disbelievers will be proved wrong.

REACHING THE SUMMIT!

Aside from the photographs of the Abominable Snowman's footprints, the other great excitement on the 1951 British expedition to Everest had been the discovery of a potential new route to the summit from the Nepalese side of the mountain.

The route, which Shipton and his team had started to explore, had some very difficult climbing at the lower level over the Khumbu Ice-fall – a long and dangerous climb with frightening, wobbly towers of ice and gaping crevasses. But, on the highest slopes – via the Western Cwm and the South Col – the route looked as though it might be more straightforward.

This meant that when the climbers' mental and physical abilities were really declining with the lack of oxygen, the route might not require such advanced climbing skills.

No one knew for sure, but there was a lot of hope that the top of Everest would be reached very soon.

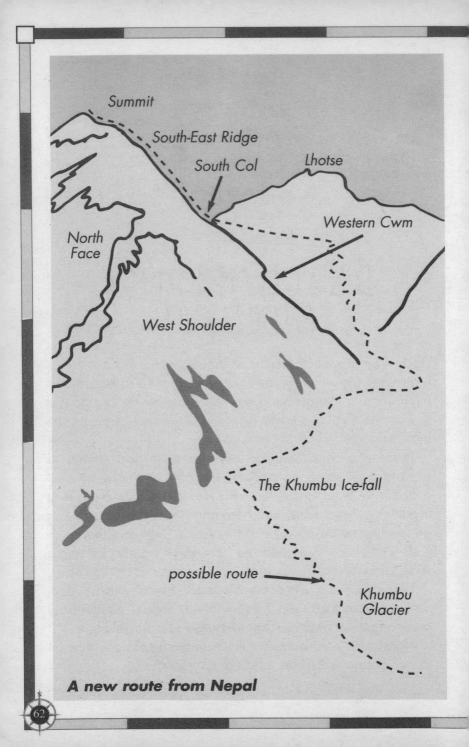

Summit

South-East Ridge

South Col

Lhotse

North Face

Western Cwm

West Shoulder

The Khumbu Ice-fall

possible route

Khumbu Glacier

A new route from Nepal

EXTREME FACTS
ICE DANGERS

Ice-falls

These are steep and dangerous sections of a glacier where its movement underneath causes a chaotic mixture of ever-shifting crevasses, walls of ice and unstable ice-towers. It is usually better to travel around the edge of an ice-fall than to try to climb over it.

However, the route discovered in 1951 includes a crossing of the Khumbu Ice-fall. This is still the most popular route to Everest today. It is a very risky part of the climb because at any moment a new crevasse can suddenly appear below you, or an unstable ice-tower can tumble down on top of you. It is one of the scariest parts of the expedition to Everest because the ground underneath your feet, or in front of you, can change so quickly. And everyone fears that one of the towers of ice might suddenly fall on them, meaning almost certain death.

Crevasses

A split or crack in the ice of a glacier, crevasses can be very shallow or they can be hundreds of metres deep. Some are narrow enough to jump across, others are far too wide to get over and climbers have to go around them. Expeditions bring special ladders to place across them. In winter and spring crevasses can be covered by snow and so are difficult to spot. To try and prevent themselves falling in, climbers usually rope themselves together and then prod their ice-axes in the snow in front of them before they move forward.

Mountaineer John Evans climbs the rope ladder at the top of the dangerous Khumbu Ice-fall

GOING FOR THE TOP

In 1953 a large British expedition, under the leadership of Colonel John Hunt, arrived in Nepal with great hopes of placing the first men on the top of Everest. A Swiss expedition the year before had got to within 244 m of the summit. It was felt that someone would definitely stand on the top of Everest very soon.

Hunt was a brilliant organizer of men and equipment and he was determined that this expedition should succeed. He insisted that all fourteen members of his climbing party should be mountaineers who had the skill and experience to reach the summit of Everest. He would decide who was physically and mentally best suited for the attempt when they were there. The climbing team included a thirty-three-year-old New Zealand bee-keeper called Edmund Hillary and the experienced Sherpa, Tenzing Norgay, an Indian citizen.

Sherpas

Sherpa is the name of a group of people from the Nepalese side of Everest, from the Khumbu region. Because they have been born and live in the high Himalayas, they are used to working in the thin air here and don't need as much acclimatization as Westerners when on the lower slopes of Everest. They work as porters and assistants on expeditions and are famous for their climbing skills and their strength. Nowadays the term Sherpa is often used to refer to anyone from the Himalayas who works as a porter. The head of the Sherpas on an expedition is called the 'Sirdar'.

Arrival
In February 1953 the team sailed from Britain to India and then flew on to Nepal. On 17 March they set out from Kathmandu with 320 people helping them carry items to Base Camp. On the way, they spent two weeks near the monastery of Thyangboche, which is 3,962 m above sea level. From here they had their first sight of Everest. Hunt made them spend the two weeks walking in these hills, climbing 6,096 m peaks to help them get used to the altitude and to carrying the oxygen equipment.

The challenge of the ice-fall

By 12 April the expedition had reached the top of the Khumbu Glacier, where they made their Base Camp. The team started making their way up the ice-fall through the ice-walls and crevasses and wobbly towers of ice. It was difficult and dangerous work.

They hacked steps out of the ice, fixed ropes over the steepest parts and set up ladders across the crevasses. Inching your way across these shaky ladders is always very frightening.

It was long and tiring work, but the men kept their spirits high – even when night-time snow falls had covered up their hard work of the previous day.

Moving upwards

After days of dangerous climbing, Advanced Base Camp was set up on the Western Cwm at 6,460 m. Over the next three weeks, teams of Sherpas and climbers carried up supplies over the route they had prepared.

Living Together

On an expedition it is very important that people get on with each other because everyone is going to be living together in cramped conditions for weeks, and perhaps months, at a time. If a team is badly selected, there are often rows and some members fall out with each other. This can lead to unease and a lack of teamwork. A good leader, and one who picks the right people, is vital to an expedition.

Selecting the summit teams

By 17 May Hunt was ready to choose his two summit assault teams. He had decided that each would have two members and be supported by others 'down below'. He selected Tom Bourdillon and John Evans for the first team and Hillary and Tenzing for the second.

All these men had proved well able to cope with the altitude, climbing and, most importantly, worked well together in their pairs. To let the two assault teams keep their strength for the hard climb ahead, the other climbers now undertook most of the carrying work.

If the first pair didn't succeed, the second would have a go. If they too didn't achieve the summit, then Hunt would consider sending up a third team, if time and weather allowed.

Right to the top

On 20 May, Evans and Bourdillon had reached the South Summit – higher than anyone else had ever been in the world! From here they could see the final part of the route. But it would probably take at least another three hours to get to the summit itself.

They had to make a very difficult decision. Earlier trouble with some of the oxygen equipment had delayed them and they now felt it was too late in the day to make the summit and back in safety. Very, very reluctantly they decided to turn back. It was a sad moment for them, to get so close and not to complete the task. They hoped Hillary and Tenzing would be more successful.

The Second Attempt

Two days later Hillary and Tenzing found themselves high on the mountain, on the South-East Ridge, looking for a spot to set up a final camp. All around the ground sloped steeply at 45 degrees. Eventually they found a little ledge under a rock-face. They could just squeeze their tent on to it. This was where they would spend the night.

The support party left their loads and set off back down to the South Col. Hillary and Tenzing then dug out two small places for themselves in the snow and put the tent over the top. They were at 8,500 m. And from the summit itself, they were only 350 m – the top of the world, the place they wanted to reach the next day. Their minds were full of thoughts: could they do it?

The night before
After a meal of sardines on biscuits, jam, honey, dates and tinned apricots (which Hillary had thawed over the stove), they went to 'bed' and tried to get some sleep.

But it wasn't a very comfortable night. There was a lot of wind outside, and inside the tiny tent they had to rest in a half sitting position, leaning against the sides of it – though this did help stop the tent from being blown away! In addition, the very high altitude made it difficult to sleep without bottled oxygen.

They had calculated that they had enough oxygen to use for four hours each during the night to help them rest. Hillary used his between 9 p.m. and 11 p.m. and between 1 p.m. and 3 a.m. With the oxygen they could doze quite well, but without it they felt miserable. When they lay awake they wondered if their ordeal was worth it.

The day dawns
But they were lucky! At 4 a.m., when Hillary and Tenzing looked out of the tent the wind had dropped and the weather was fine.

It was still dark and the temperature was way below freezing point – not easy to get out of bed! But this could be the most important day of their lives and they started to struggle out of their sleeping-bags into the bitterly cold air.

It took them two and a half hours to get ready to leave. Their morning tasks included lighting the stove, making tea, eating sardines on biscuits again and drinking lots of lemon juice and sugar.

In addition Hillary had to thaw out his boots. They had frozen solid overnight. There was a strong smell of burning leather in the tent as he held them over the stove!

By the time they were ready to leave the tent they were wearing all the clothes they had with them on this lonely mountain top – including special down clothing, windproof outer garments and three pairs of gloves each (silk, woollen and windproof). They then checked their oxygen equipment and were relieved to find it seemed to be working fine.

At 6.30 a.m. they crawled out of the tent on to the snow, put the oxygen gear on to their backs (14 kg in weight) and set off. They were really on their way now! Perhaps today would be the day ...

Making steps

Tenzing led first, kicking steps into the snow. Slowly they made their way towards the ridge. The snow was quite soft and therefore not very secure. This meant there was a great threat of avalanches. They stopped to decide what to do. Should they continue on? It was dangerous territory.

After a brief discussion, they decided to continue. By 9 a.m. they had reached the South Summit. Bourdillon and Evans had stood here two days before. If Hillary and Tenzing continued, they would tread where no person had set foot before!

A rest

With relief they sat down and had a snack and a drink – and looked at the route in front. Even if it hadn't been at altitude, the ridge would have been difficult. On the side overhanging the Kangshung Face a false step would send them sliding thousands of metres to their deaths on the glacier below. On the other side there was a steep drop of about 2,440 m to the Western Cwm.

Onwards and upwards

They moved on. As they cut steps with an ice-axe, they were relieved to find that the snow here was firm Hillary was now in front, cutting the steps. They stayed roped together, Tenzing belaying in case Hillary slipped. These steps were also going to be important when they were on their return journey and tired. They had to be as secure as possible for their bulky climbing boots.

Making Ice Steps

Cutting steps into the ice and snow on the side of a mountain takes a lot of time and energy – especially in Everest's Death Zone. Nowadays ropes are fixed at the beginning of the season to help climbers. Hillary and Tenzing had to do it all themselves.

Oxygen danger

Thousands of metres below the two men could see the tents of the camp in the Western Cwm – just tiny dots. Then Hillary realized that Tenzing had slowed down and was having trouble breathing. He moved over to him to check his oxygen equipment. It was so cold that icicles had frozen in the tube to Tenzing's face mask, blocking his supply. Hillary managed to clear it and immediately Tenzing could breathe freely. Hillary then checked his own tube. Ice was building up here too and needed clearing to stop him having similar difficulties. From then on they both kept a much closer check to stop this frightening situation occurring again.

A rocky barrier

After about an hour they came to a steep 12 m high rock cliff. They already knew from aerial photographs that this obstacle was here – and they also knew that it could be the very thing that might still stop them getting to the summit. Hillary later said:

'The rock itself, smooth and almost holdless, might have been an interesting Sunday afternoon problem to a group of expert rock climbers in the Lake District, but here it was a barrier beyond our feeble strength to overcome.'

Remember they were now at almost 8,800 m. There seemed no route around it to the west side, and on the east side there were several great cornices of snow lying against it. Was it going to be impossible to get past this cliff?

Cornices

A cornice is an overhanging 'wave-crest' of snow. The high winds that whip around mountains form the snow into peaks like the crests of waves that overhang the firmer snow, ice and rock below. Sometimes cornices can be climbed, but they are often very dangerous and should be avoided if at all possible.

Suddenly Hillary spotted a narrow gap between the rock and one of the cornices on the right-hand side, the side above the Kangshung Face:

'I jammed my way into this crack, then kicking backwards with my crampons I sank their spikes deep into the frozen snow behind me and levered myself off the ground. Taking advantage of every little rock hold and all the force of knee, shoulder and arms I could muster, I literally cramponed backwards up the crack, with a fervent prayer that the cornice would remain attached to the rock.'

And it did hold! At the top he flopped down with exhaustion – it had been a shattering climb. He was panting breathlessly. But he was full of excitement. For the first time he really felt that nothing now could stop them from reaching the top of Everest – they might really make it.

Tenzing followed him up and collapsed too. He also had the amazing feeling that they could do it!

The ridge

But they still had a way to go. And they still had to be very careful on this treacherous ridge. One false step and they could fall to their deaths a very, very, long way below.

They checked their oxygen equipment again and continued on. The ridge curved away in front of them. Every time they came round one hump, another, higher one appeared in front of them. They started by cramponing steps, but quickly realized that they needed to cut larger steps with the ice-axe. But this was so, so tiring. Hillary was shattered after two hours of this exhausting work. His arms and back ached. He and Tenzing had now lost the glow of excitement they had had on completing the climb of the rock step. It was becoming a real struggle to keep going.

They also felt dull and lifeless from the lack of oxygen. Where was the summit? Would they ever get there? Could they ever get there?

The end in sight

Hillary continued cutting steps in a tired, dull and almost robot-like state. He had to concentrate even harder than before. He just made himself keep going. In this state it came as a sudden shock to look up and find that they were, at last, only a final few steps from the summit itself.

'I then realized that the ridge ahead, instead of still monotonously rising, now dropped sharply away, and far below I could see the North Col and the Rongbuk Glacier. I looked upwards to see a narrow stone ridge running to a snowy summit. A few more whacks of the ice-axe in the firm snow and we stood on top.'

They had made it! Hillary and Tenzing had reached the top of the world! The first people ever to be there!

The summit itself!

It was 11.30 a.m. The ridge had taken them two and a half hours – a very, very long two and a half hours. Hillary's first feeling was one of huge relief. He looked at Tenzing,

'... in spite of the balaclava, goggles and oxygen mask all encrusted with long icicles that concealed his face, there was no disguising his infectious grin of pure delight as he looked all around him.'

Hillary and Tenzing shook hands and then Tenzing flung his arms around Hillary's shoulders. They thumped each other on the back. Below lay the other mountains and ranges of the Himalayas very clearly defined, like a great relief map.

The world-famous shot of an exhilarated Tenzing, standing on the summit for the very first time in 1953.

The Summit

The summit of Everest is surprisingly small. Sir Chris Bonington (a British mountaineer who climbed Everest in 1985) said it was the same size as a pool table! In the 1970s the Chinese put a tripod on the top of Everest and this was there for many years, marking the summit. Now it has disappeared, probably blown away.

MAKING HISTORY

The two men could look down into Nepal and into Tibet. Hillary looked down to the North Ridge and towards the North Col – the same route that Mallory and Irvine had taken. He looked around the summit to see if there was any sign that these earlier climbers had been there. There was no evidence – but thirty years on it would probably have been destroyed anyway by the weather.

Hillary turned off his oxygen and removed his set. He took out his camera (which he had been carrying inside his shirt to keep it warm) and asked Tenzing to pose for him on the top of the mountain, holding his ice-axe with the flags of Britain, Nepal, India and the United Nations tied to it. This was to become one of the most famous photographs ever taken in the history of humankind – it has appeared in newspapers, magazines and books throughout the world ever since. It was to mark 29 May 1953 as a day to remember for ever.

Hillary then took photographs of all the ridges leading to the summit to prove they had actually been there – there are many doubting critics in this world.

While Hillary was taking the photographs, Tenzing was burying some offerings to the Himalayan gods in the snow – some sweets, a chocolate bar and a packet of biscuits. Alongside, Hillary buried a small Christian crucifix which Hunt had asked him to place at the top. Now the gods had been attended to, they ate some mint cake to revive themselves.

They knew they shouldn't stay long at the summit. They needed to get going so they could reach the reserves of oxygen they had left beneath the South Summit before their own supplies ran out. When Hillary had put his oxygen back on he had immediately felt less dull and clumsy – everything seemed to shine brighter too.

So after fifteen minutes on the summit, they left. They knew they had to be very careful. Going down a mountain can often be the most dangerous part. Once climbers have reached their goal they sometimes stop concentrating so hard on their climbing, which, combined with tiredness, can mean severe trouble.

Getting down

They cramponed back along the ridge, via the tracks they had made shortly before with so much effort. Then they went down the rock step (now known as the Hillary Step) and slowly over the snow to the South Summit.

Here they paused to refresh themselves with a sweetened lemon drink before they carefully picked their way along the dangerous snow slope leading down to the Kangshung Glacier.

At 2 p.m. they got back to their little tent on its tiny ledge. Even the lightish winds of that day had loosened it from some of its fastenings. They lit the stove and made themselves another hot lemon drink with lots of sugar. They now felt very weak and exhausted. Yesterday they had been working here without oxygen, but today, after reaching the summit, even with oxygen they felt shattered.

Signs of life

They could see figures moving down below them on the South Col. They picked up their sleeping-bags and air mattresses and tied them to their oxygen frames to use at the South Col camp. It took an enormous effort to get themselves going again, but they managed to stir themselves to set off.

Down, down they kept going. When they reached the last stage they found the wind, which had been getting stronger and stronger, had blown snow across their original steps and they were now looking at a hard frozen slope. So they had to start cutting steps again – otherwise they would not be able to descend this part safely. Hillary chipped away for 60 m, then Tenzing took over. The wind was now flinging itself at them in strong gusts, trying to throw them off the mountain. As they reached more stable snow, they were able to stop cutting and, with relief, went back to the easier task of kicking out a track again – though this was still hard work for men in their state of exhaustion.

Towards camp

They continued on down the long slope above the South Col. Then, about 30 m above the camp, a team member came out to meet them with hot soup and more oxygen. He was so excited by their news – but Hillary and Tenzing had no energy left to celebrate. They just crawled into the tent and collapsed. Hillary's last oxygen cylinder, in fact, ran out just before they reached the tents – he'd just had enough to do it, but only just!

That night a wild gale blew around their tents on the South Col and the temperature dropped.

The next morning, as they made their way on down with their support team, Hillary and Tenzing were shattered. They moved slowly and kept having to stop for rests. Hunt was overjoyed when he heard the news of their success. All the efforts of the team had been worthwhile.

Coronation triumph

The news of Hillary and Tenzing's summit success reached England in time for Queen Elizabeth II's coronation – on Monday, 2 June 1953. The papers were full of it. *The Times* wrote:

THEIR VICTORY IS A VICTORY FOR THE HUMAN SPIRIT

The whole world rejoiced. Hillary – a very modest man – was astonished that he had become so famous. The success of climbing the highest mountain in the world had grabbed the attention and imagination of people across the globe from all walks of life. It was a brave and daring triumph.

Sir Edmund Hillary and the Himalayas

Since 1953 Hillary has helped to raise a great deal of money to build more than a dozen hospitals and schools in Nepal. He also helped create Sagarmatha National Park which surrounds Everest.

TEAMWORK

Hillary, Tenzing, Hunt and all the other expedition members got rewards from all over the world. The men had worked extremely well together for over four months in very difficult and dangerous conditions. Hunt felt this excellent team spirit and unity was the ultimate key to Hillary and Tenzing's success – he felt it was even more important than good equipment or good food. All these things combined to link in with the one thing they had no control over – the weather. The expedition was lucky – the day Hillary and Tenzing reached the top there was not much wind. Good teamwork, good weather, good organization and good equipment had all contributed to their record-breaking success.

Mountaineer Dougal Haston climbs the Hillary Step. Named after Sir Edmund Hillary, this difficult ridge is the final challenge to be overcome before reaching the summit (via the South-East Ridge route).

EVEREST ADVENTURE

OTHER GREAT FIRSTS

Since Hillary and Tenzing successfully summited Everest in 1953, there have been a number of other 'great firsts'. The summit has been reached from other directions and some of these climbs have been technically extremely difficult. Those who first succeeded on these various climbs have been well recognized in the mountaineering world – see the Timeline on page 117 for details of these.

Among the great Everest firsts that have excited the imagination of the general public are the first ascent by a woman and the first ascents without bottled oxygen. All the climbers who took part in those faced the challenge of a lifetime as they attempted their own personal assaults on the highest mountain in the world.

THE FIRST WOMAN TO CLIMB EVEREST

For many years expeditions to Everest were all-male ones, although sometimes Nepalese women were among the porters who carried supplies to Base Camp. Then, from the 1950s, a few women began to take part in expeditions, but there were none included in any summit team.

It wasn't until 1975 that a woman actually reached the top of Everest – thirty-five-year-old Junko Tabei from Japan.

Junko was an experienced mountaineer. She had spent many years climbing in Japan and in 1970 had been part of an all-women team to climb Annapurna III (7,555 m) in the Himalayas. The following year she was invited to be the climbing leader of an all-female expedition to Everest. She was keen to take on this challenge but, as she was now married, she was expected by Japanese society to be an obedient wife and stay at home to look after her husband.

Fortunately for Junko, her husband (also a climber) supported her mountaineering ambitions. However, he made one condition – she must have a baby first! When, in April 1972, the women's team applied to Nepal for official permission for the expedition, Junko was four months' pregnant. When she set off on the expedition in spring 1975 her daughter, Noriko, was nearly two and a half. Junko had kept her side of the bargain!

Preparations

Like all expeditions, the team had to take a great deal of time to prepare and get sponsors. It was not easy convincing Japanese companies that they should sponsor an all-women expedition. But eventually Junko and the rest of the team managed to raise the money they needed and get all their equipment organized.

Sponsors

Sponsors are people or companies who give money and/or equipment to an expedition. Often they expect some publicity in return – e.g., a photograph of their equipment on the mountain, or of a banner with the company name on it flying from the summit.

Before she left, Junko made a tape-recording of herself with her daughter to leave as a memento for her young child in case she did not return alive. She and her husband were well aware of the potential dangers of climbing Everest. She wanted her daughter to have this memory of their time together in case the worst happened.

Base Camp

On 16 March 1975 the expedition set up their Base Camp. By early May, despite bad weather, they had established camps up to the South Col.

But then the weather worsened even more and they decided to retreat to three camps below to sit out the storms. On the morning of 4 May they woke up to the sound of an ominous, loud rumbling noise. It was an avalanche!

Avalanche!

Everything was so sudden. Their tents were hit by a wall of snow and immediately Junko found she could not move. She felt the snow was crushing her. And someone was lying on top of her too. She yelled out. There was no reply, only silence. As she struggled against unconsciousness she thought of her daughter – she must not die, her daughter needed her.

Rescue

The next thing Junko was aware of was lying outside the tent, on top of the snow. Her body was free of the crush. Beside her she heard someone praying. She opened her eyes, she was alive!

Later she found that seven of the Japanese team had been hurt and six of the Sherpas. The roaring avalanche had also hit their tents. Luckily, some of the other Sherpas had managed to pull them out. Junko was the worst injured – her legs were badly bruised and her hip bones had been stretched as she had been pulled out by her legs. But she had survived.

There was now pressure put on Junko to go back to Base Camp to recover. But Junko would have none of that. She refused because she knew that there was not enough time to go down, recover, climb up again to this point and then make a summit attempt before the monsoon started. She was determined that this women's team would conquer Everest, and that she would be part of it if at all possible. Three days later she was up and about and walking again.

On 10 May the expedition leader announced the summit assault party – Junko's name was included!

Climbing up

By 15 May Junko and her summit partner, the expedition Sirdar, Ang Tschering, had reached over 8,500 m. Here they cut away ice with their axes to make a level space to set up their tent for the night.

Junko said that the Sirdar behaved like a perfect gentleman when she had to go to the toilet. He held the rope that was attached to her from inside the tent so he couldn't see her. She needed to be tied to the rope in case she slipped. This is common mountaineering practice in dangerous areas, such as in high camps on bad slopes like this.

EVEREST TOILET TRIPS

Going to the toilet on Everest is difficult for various reasons:
- You have to be careful you don't get frostbite on your exposed areas.
- On a steep slope, you must make sure you are tied on to someone or something in case you slip. Some people have fallen to their deaths in this way.

A WORD OF ADVICE:

Don't pee too near to your camp. You might accidentally pick up the snow the following morning to heat water for your morning tea!

British mountaineer Sir Chris Bonington once said: 'Oh the absolute lethargy of 24,600 ft. You want to pee, and you lie there for a quarter of an hour making up your mind to look for the pee bottle.'
But male mountaineers are lucky – at least they can use pee bottles as they lie in the warmth of their sleeping-bags in their tents. Women have to get up and go outside into the cold!

Nowadays at Everest Base Camps the toilet wastes are removed – by lorries in Tibet and by porters in Nepal. Part of the money climbers pay for their expeditions goes towards funding this. At the permanent higher camps, climbers usually burn their toilet paper.

On further

The next morning the pair made their way through deep powdered snow to the South Summit. Then they followed the narrow ridge towards the real summit, at times traversing below it on the Nepalese side using the top of it as a handhold. Junko commented later that if she looked over the top here her head was in Tibet and her chest in Nepal! A slip here would mean certain death.

They reached the Hillary Step (see page 77). This, difficult in good conditions, was now covered in ice with fresh snow lying on top – a very dangerous climb. But Junko and Ang Tschering got over it and continued on slowly, taking many rests in the high altitude.

At the top!

On 16 May 1975 Junko became the first woman to stand on the top of Everest. It was only twelve days since the avalanche had trapped her. She was a determined lady!

Everest women

The year 1975 was appropriately International Women's Year, especially as just eleven days after Junko another woman made it to the summit – Phantog, a thirty-seven-year-old Tibetan member of a joint Chinese-Tibetan expedition. She had climbed from the other side via the North Col and the North-East Ridge. In doing so she lost three toes to frostbite, but she too had proved that woman mountaineers should be accepted on the world's highest mountain. Women have been climbing Everest ever since.

EXTREME FACTS
FROSTBITE

Frostbite happens when the tissues in part of the body freeze in very cold conditions. To conserve heat, the body withdraws blood to its centre to keep the most important organs, such as the heart and the lungs, warm. This is why frostbite most usually affects the hands, feet, nose and ears as the blood supply to these parts becomes very poor.

At first someone with frostbite does not sense any pain, maybe just a lack of feeling in the limb – the frostbitten part is pale and numb. Then, if still badly frozen, the affected area will become dull-purple and difficult to move. If it becomes a dark-purple this means it is very badly damaged indeed. The part can then blacken and

A case of severe frostbite, following the first ascent of Everest's North Face.

come away from the body, or if it becomes gangrenous it will have to be amputated (cut off).

Protection

There are a variety of ways to help protect the body from frostbite:

- keep wind off the hands and feet, with good gloves and boots
- wear loose but well-insulated clothing
- don't get wet
- don't touch metal with bare fingers
- look out for signs of numbness

NO EXTRA OXYGEN

One of the most remarkable feats on Everest was the first ascent without extra bottled oxygen – especially as no one knew if it was possible to do this and come back alive or, even if alive, without permanent brain damage.

In 1978 two men were brave enough to try for the summit of Everest without bottled oxygen supplies – Italian Reinhold Messner and Austrian Peter Habeler. Before they attempted Everest they had already climbed several peaks over 8,000 m without bottled oxygen. Everest was to be the big one!

On 8 May they left their South Col camp at 5 a.m.

The climb
About four hours later, they were at their next camp, at 8,500 m.

Here they brewed some tea (a process which took half an hour) and watched as the weather seemed to get worse. They sat in silence, but the silence of true companions. Both felt – independently of the other – that it would be tempting to stay there in the comfort of the tent, but they knew that if they did so they would never have the strength to continue upwards later. They knew that even if they only made it to the South Summit they would have proved that it was probably possible to climb to the very top of Everest itself without bottled oxygen. They both had to go on.

Habeler and Messner had talked about what they would do if one of them got into severe difficulties. They had agreed that if this happened the other man should try and save only himself. Without any extra oxygen it was clear that if one tried to help the other in a crisis, both would probably die. They were firm friends and had climbed together before at altitude without bottled oxygen. They both knew the risks of what they were attempting.

The South Summit
Deep snow now lay in their way and they had to make a detour towards the South-East Ridge. One false step here and they would have fallen 2,000 m down the steep drop. Yet the two skilled climbers made their way through here in safety and at last came out above the clouds on to the South Summit.

Storm
They were almost immediately hit by the storm that had been threatening for a while. Yet, strangely, they both felt stronger because they were now nearer their final goal – the summit itself. And, although they didn't speak to each other, they later discovered that it was here, on the South Summit in this storm, that they both felt certain they would get to the top.

Grim faces

They could each see that the other was really suffering without the extra bottled oxygen. They both had terrible grimaces on their faces caused by their mouths hanging open continuously while they gasped for air. Icicles hung from their beards, giving them a strange monstrous appearance. The pair were quite a scary sight!

They were so exhausted that they could hardly move more than a few paces without stopping to rest. Although they had roped themselves together, they knew that, on the summit ridge, if one slipped, the reactions of the other would be too slow to save them both.

Dream-like

The world without enough oxygen was strange and dream-like. They were almost in a trance – and this made them feel the mountain was their friend. Everything seemed really positive. However, at this time they were closer to death than at any other on the ascent.

They moved along like robots. Habeler felt as though he had stepped out of his body and that he was watching someone else walking in his place. This other man pulled himself up the Hillary Step. This other man had one foot above the 2,000 m drop to Nepal on the left and the 4,000 m drop to Tibet on the right. This extra man seemed even more real than his human climbing companion, Messner. In fact, he no longer thought of Messner.

Habeler saw his other self crawling forward on hands and knees, slowly, painfully making his way to the summit.

The summit

Suddenly Habeler realized he was standing up. He was standing up on the summit itself! Then Messner appeared behind him. They hugged each other. They cried. They had made it. Their tears froze on their cheeks. They were the first people to reach the top of Everest without bottled oxygen! It could be done!

WITHOUT BOTTLED OXYGEN – AND ALONE

The first man

But this great first was not enough for Messner. Now he wanted a new challenge – to get to the top of Everest without bottled oxygen on his own.

On 17 August 1980 he began his climb from his Advanced Base Camp on the Rongbuk Glacier, on the Tibetan side of the mountain. He carried everything he would need in a rucksack – a little tent, a sleeping-bag, a mattress, a stove, food and a camera.

On the second night he camped at 8,200 m. After climbing all day in the thin air without extra oxygen, he found it difficult to summon the energy even to eat and drink.

Early the next morning he looked out of his tent and saw clouds, but he was determined to continue. He had breakfast, drank some lukewarm water and set out upwards again, leaving his tent and most of his equipment behind.

Each moment

Messner found that he was not thinking about the top but about each moment as it happened. Each and every movement he made. Each piece of ice, rock and snow as he moved over it. He was almost not in charge of his body. He just kept going, going, going. At times on his lonely climb he had felt that there was someone else with him – a feeling that often happened to him when he climbed at this altitude. He found it strangely comforting.

Monotonously, automatically, he carried on. Suddenly, and surprisingly, he found himself there, on the summit. His mind was so tired he couldn't even react with any emotion. His body too was totally shattered. But he had made it – the first person to climb Everest with no bottled oxygen, totally alone! He later admitted:

'I was in continual agony; I have never in my life been so tired as on the summit of Everest that day. I just sat and sat there, oblivious to everything ...'

The Greatest Mountaineer Ever?

A few years after his solo ascent of Everest without bottled oxygen, Messner became the first person to climb all fourteen peaks in the world higher than 8,000 m. Some people think he is the greatest mountaineer ever.

The first woman

The first woman to climb Everest alone and without bottled oxygen was British mountaineer Alison Hargreaves. She reached the summit on 13 May 1995, having climbed the treacherous North Ridge. She carried her own tent, food and other supplies with her.

Tragically, Alison Hargreaves was killed just three months later in an avalanche on K2.

There is a fine line between success and disaster in the high mountains of the Himalayas.

Mallory's Grandson

In 1995 the thirty-five-year-old grandson of the famous Everest climber Mallory (see page 30), also called George Mallory, climbed to the summit of Everest along the same route his relative had taken seventy-one years before.

SKIING FROM THE SUMMIT

In 2000 a thirty-eight-year-old extreme sports enthusiast, Slovenian Davo Karnicar, climbed to the summit of Everest in order to ski down. It was an incredibly dangerous idea and many people considered him completely mad. Karnicar had a camera on his safety helmet and others had been placed on the mountain at good viewing points along his route. Thousands of people around the world saw the event live via the Internet, watching as he skied down over the ice and snow, trying to avoid all those rocks and boulders. His most frightening moments were when he felt stretches of ice collapse beneath him. He knew any moment he could be lying dead at the bottom of an enormous crevasse.

But the Internet watchers breathed a sigh of relief when he made it safely. It had taken him just five hours!

EVEREST DANGERS

There are many dangers on Everest – from the weather, the altitude, the extreme cold, avalanches and crevasses to very, very steep drops. Dangerous situations also occur because of human tiredness and human mistakes.

The good mountaineer comes to Everest as prepared as possible for anything to happen. But all experienced climbers know that luck – good and bad – will always play a part in any attempt on the summit.

There are many stories of climbers dealing with Everest dangers. Some end happily, some tragically. Here are just three.

Avalanche!

In 1984 the British mountaineer Brummie Stokes was the joint leader of an SAS expedition to climb the North Face. He had already climbed Everest by the South Col with a British army expedition in 1976 and on that occasion had lost several of his toes to frostbite.

On the evening of 24 March 1984 the team members settled into their sleeping-bags in their Advanced Base Camp on the Rongbuk Glacier. Everything seemed very peaceful.

However, during the night the wind blew up. The tents were in a sheltered spot so the climbers were undisturbed.

About 6.15 a.m., as he was getting up, Stokes heard someone scream an avalanche warning. There was no time to do anything. A chunk of ice whizzed through the tent, past his face and out the other side. Then his whole world turned upside down.

Trapped by snow

The entire tent was picked up and tossed down the mountain by what seemed like an enormous wind. Stokes was still inside it, tumbling around violently with all his equipment. He was screaming in panic and he was convinced he was going to die.

In among the chaos and confusion he suddenly spotted the tear in the tent made by the ice chunk. Thinking quickly, he ripped it open and struggled out just before tonnes of snow began to pile down on top of him. Then he lost consciousness.

Luckily, he must have come to almost immediately. The next thing he was aware of was fighting against the snow. He felt it was suffocating him, but he managed to pull himself out. When he did emerge, the wind was so strong he could hardly stand up. He was horrified when he looked around him. The scene was like a battlefield. In every direction there were blocks of ice, chunks of snow and scattered equipment from the camp.

Fears

He heard a low rumbling noise and was again blown over by a terrific blast of wind. Stokes was terrified. He knew it meant another avalanche was approaching. This time he might not survive. Luckily for him, this second avalanche was heading in another direction. As relief swept over him, he noticed a figure in the distance waving at him. Stokes realized he was asking for an axe. Why? He turned around to look in the remains of his tent.

More dangers

As he turned his head, he felt a sharp hot pain in his neck, far worse than any pain he had ever felt. He slumped to his knees with the agony. But he knew he must go to help his colleague. He struggled to search the contents of his half-buried tent in vain. He could see no ice-axe, so he struggled over to his team mate without one.

Then he felt the snow give way as a crevasse opened up underneath him. The fear of death hit him again. But yet again he was lucky. The crevasse was not too deep. Somehow he summoned up the strength from his shattered body to pull himself out.

Rescue

Stokes reached his colleague and saw why he needed an ice-axe. He wanted to free someone whose head was trapped under a block of ice.

In his desperation, Stokes pulled a plastic spoon from his pocket and started scraping at the snow around the ice. The man was still conscious but very dazed. Eventually they managed to free him.

Tragically, however, as they searched further, they found that another climber had died.

Aftermath

They were all in a state of shock. Stokes radioed their Base Camp to tell them what had happened. His voice shaking, he begged them to send up a rescue team with tents and sleeping bags.

It was just after 7 a.m., less than an hour from when he'd been putting on his boots.

STRANDED

Getting to the summit of Everest is only the halfway point in the expedition. Returning to Advanced Base Camp can often be more dangerous, especially as a climber is then very tired and suffering more and more from the high altitude.

There have been several occasions when climbers have not been able to reach their Advanced Base Camp. They have had to spend the night near the summit without tents (an emergency bivouac). This happens because the climbers have been delayed, a moonless night has fallen, or because the weather has become so bad it is impossible to see or even move. Some have survived this ordeal and returned to tell their tale. Others have been less fortunate.

EXTREME FACTS
EMERGENCY BIVOUAC

A bivouac (or 'bivi') is a temporary camp made in an emergency, usually for a night. For planned bivouacs climbers usually have with them with them a tent or a bivouac sack (a special light body-size bag) as well as a stove, food and additional clothing. But in emergencies bivouacs can be a horrendous experience, especially if the conditions are very cold. The most important things are to conserve heat and to get shelter. Often the mountaineer needs to dig into the snow by a rock to escape the wind. Up on

Everest there is no guarantee that someone will survive the night.

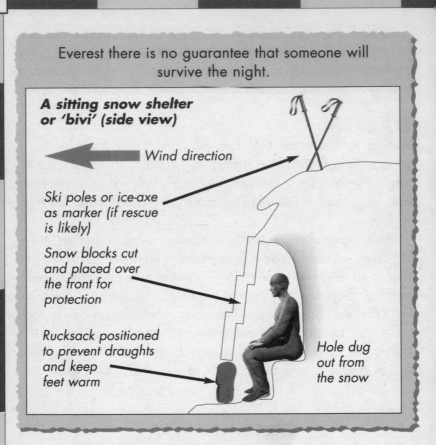

A *sitting snow shelter* or 'bivi' (side view)

← Wind direction

Ski poles or ice-axe as marker (if rescue is likely)

Snow blocks cut and placed over the front for protection

Rucksack positioned to prevent draughts and keep feet warm

Hole dug out from the snow

Lost on the mountain

On 12 May 1988 British climber Stephen Venables reached the summit at 3.40 p.m. He had been climbing without porters or bottled oxygen via a new route up the Kangshung Face. Although he had started with two American companions, he reached the summit on his own. The others had turned back due to extreme exhaustion.

Venables only spent ten minutes on the summit. He knew it was very late in the day to start down and he was already hours behind schedule. It would be dark soon. The weather was threatening to change. Venables was alone and he had

Doug Scott on the Everest summit, following the first ascent of the South-West Face in 1975. After this photo was taken, he and Dougal Haston had to make an emergency bivouac as it was too late for them to descend.

chosen to climb without oxygen. Would he ever get back to camp that night?

He set off but after a while he realized he was heading too far to the right. He was going down towards the South-West Face. A climber could easily walk off the edge here, just as others had done before.

He changed direction. Now he seemed to be over to the left, too near to the drop over the Kangshung Face. To no avail, he tried to find his own tracks. He so much wanted to rest that he sank down into the snow. The temptation to stay there was overwhelming, but it would have meant certain death through hypothermia. Venables struggled up and continued on.

He took off his mittens to attach his belt clip to the fixed rope on the Hillary Step. He managed to pull them on again and started abseiling down. At the bottom he collapsed on the edge of the ridge, panting furiously. He couldn't fill his lungs and he felt as if he was suffocating. Gradually his breathing returned to normal.

A strange companion

Venables stumbled on. As he did, he became aware of an old man by his side. In the thick snow swirling in front of him he could see very little, but somehow he made it to the South Summit. Here he collapsed, gasping for breath. However, he was more concerned about the old man, who was having similar difficulties.

Together they descended the knife-edge ridge and then started to slide towards the safety of the South Col. Then the old man got very frightened. They were going faster and faster, setting off mini-avalanches.

Venables dug in his heels and leaned hard on his ice-axe, to slow down. They stopped to rest. Venables found a place to cut a ledge and then he collapsed. He was exhausted and confused and it was nearly dark.

A while later (possibly an hour), he decided it was too dangerous a spot to spend the night and he tried to carry on. He didn't know where he was. It was now dark and because there was no moon it was very difficult to see, even with his head-torch on. Venables began to worry that he had missed the point to turn right into the couloir leading to the camp.

Emergency bivouac

The old man then suggested they stop where they were and wait until the morning. Venables dug an emergency bivouac in the snow on a ledge. It was about 9 p.m. They had to do their best in order to stay alive during the long night ahead.

Fortunately the wind had dropped and the air temperature was now about −30°C. Venables was sheltered. He was wearing warm clothes. Maybe he would lose some toes to frostbite, but if that were all, he would be lucky. He had not intended to stay the night on the mountain, so he had no stove to melt snow. There was only a trickle of half-frozen orange juice in his water bottle. He was very dehydrated − in the last twenty-four hours he had drunk less than a litre.

Company

But he was not alone. The old man was still there. And then other people came crowding on to the tiny ledge, people who warmed his hands for a while.

As he lay there, Venables drifted in and out of his dream-like state. Towards dawn all his companions, apart from the old man, left, saying they were going to see some yak herders camped around the corner. Venables knew there couldn't be any yak herders at this great height, but when they returned and said they'd had hot baths and food, he was very jealous. He desperately wanted to be warm.

Daybreak

Venables must have dozed off because he remembers awaking to see the grey light of dawn appearing in the sky. All the people, including the old man, had gone. His body was stiff and his feet were dead. Large lumps of ice were sticking to his eyebrows, moustache and beard. An icy film covered his nose.

And, in the early light he could see, just below his ledge, the right turn into the couloir!

Slowly and wobbly he got up. He picked up his ice-axe and started off down the slope, sliding now and again. Once he went too fast and had another frightening, suffocating, gasping fit. But then he made himself go more slowly. He eventually reached the safety of the camp.

Ultimately Venables lost three toes from frostbite. But at least he had returned alive. The old man and the people who had seemed so real to him had been figures conjured up from his imagination. Despite being imaginary, they had perked him up and helped him to stay alive.

Dream People

It is not unusual for mountaineers climbing alone in tough conditions to think that they have a companion. Not only the lack of oxygen but also the extreme physical and mental stress can cause people to imagine things. Mountaineer Messner believes the worst problem of coping with high-altitude climbing is the loneliness. He has said:

'Humans should not be up there ... If you are alone, this other person helps you to survive.'

This is not a modern experience. Frank Smythe was on the

1933 Everest expedition. He later wrote:

'I remember constantly glancing back over my shoulder, and once when, after reaching my highest point, I stopped to try and eat some mint cake, I carefully divided it and turned round with one half in my hand. It was almost a shock to find no one to whom to give it.'

Solo sailors on long voyages have also had similar experiences.

SUMMIT STORM

A terrible tragedy took place in 1996 in the Death Zone.

EXTREME FACTS
THE DEATH ZONE

The Death Zone is the top part of Everest above 8,000 m. It is the part of the mountain where:
- most deaths occur
- it is impossible to send in a rescue helicopter
- climbers are most likely to suffer from altitude sickness, tiredness and confusion
- climbers should only spend three days at most, otherwise their bodies slowly begin to get weaker from the lack of oxygen.

A climber on Everest has to be prepared for everything and should be able to take care of himself or herself if things go wrong. Above 8,000 m, even experienced altitude climbers – guides and Sherpas – are so exhausted in the thin air that it is difficult for them to help another person.

Timing on summit day is all-important. If someone finds that they are behind schedule and that there is no chance of reaching the top by 2 p.m., they should turn back. Climbers know that they should trust their gut instincts to turn back when the conditions look bad. However, as they draw near to the summit, even experienced mountaineers find its lure can overcome their common sense.

The consequences can be fatal.

Commercial climbs

Until 1985 only 187 people had managed to summit Everest. Since then, more and more people have been attempting to get to the top. By the year 2000 over 1,000 summit ascents had been made.

Many of these more recent climbers have paid a great deal of money to go on what are called commercial expeditions. The guides in charge organize all the permits, equipment and food and arrange for the higher camps to be set up by Sherpas. The 'clients' take all their directions from their guide because many have limited mountaineering experience.

The adventure of a lifetime

Many people now seem to regard climbing Everest as an exciting thing you can do if you have enough money. They think that if you have a good guide and ready-made camps, there will be few problems.

But it must be remembered that even guides can get altitude sickness and illnesses which can affect their judgement. If bad weather is added to this, a situation can quickly turn into a disaster – as happened in 1996 when eight people died in the Death Zone in a terrible storm.

TOURIST TRAGEDY

The morning of Friday, 10 May 1996 dawned bright and clear. However, members of two commercial expeditions run by Adventure Consultants and Mountain Madness had already been climbing since midnight with the help of head-torches. A rope line had been fixed up for them over the most difficult parts. The climbers clipped themselves on to the rope for safety.

Because of the lack of oxygen above the South Col, the last 900 m to the summit are more exhausting than any others on the route, even if the climbing itself is not as technically difficult as crossing the Khumbu Ice-fall lower down.

The climbers all knew it was going to be a very long, tiring day, but they had no idea that some of them would not return alive.

Oxygen supplies

The climbers were all carrying two bottles of oxygen. They were due to pick up a third bottle at the South Summit on their return. Each bottle should last five to six hours. This meant that by 4 or 5 p.m. everyone would have run out of oxygen. But by this time, if all went according to plan, they would be back, or almost back, at the camp on the South Col.

Both Adventure Consultants and Mountain Madness had eight clients each. These men and women had paid as much as $65,000 for the experience. There was also a Taiwanese expedition aiming for the summit on the same day.

So a large number of people were making for the top all at the same time. Some turned back before the South Summit, thinking it unlikely they would get to the summit on time. The rest pushed on, despite their great tiredness.

The summit
Soon after 1 p.m. the first climbers arrived at the summit. Even those who had made good progress to start with had been delayed, waiting for others to catch up or for the ropes to be fixed up in front of them.

Among those who were first to the summit was American journalist Jon Krakauer, with Adventure Consultants. He didn't stay long on the top because he was worried his bottled oxygen would run out before he got back to the South Summit.

The Hillary Step
Fifteen minutes later he had returned to the Hillary Step. Here he had to stop and wait for over an hour before he could climb down it. There was only one rope down its 12 m drop and people on their way up were using it. Krakauer could do nothing but wait and watch the queue of tired climbers struggle up the rope over the last big obstacle before the summit.

It was a terrible delay for Krakauer. While he was waiting, his oxygen supply ran out. He was at 8,800 m. Dizzy and frightened, he thought he might black out before he reached the South Summit.

The South Summit
Luckily, another climber helped him, guide Mike Groom, who shared his oxygen for the last stretch. By the time they left the South Summit – with another Adventure Consultants client, a Japanese lady, Yasuko Namba – it was 3.30 p.m. The three of them found themselves descending into thick clouds and light snow. It was very difficult to see anything.

Groom gave Krakauer (a reasonably experienced climber) permission to go on alone because Namba was moving slowly and conditions were worsening. Above their heads there were bright flashes of lightning and loud cracks of thunder. The Death Zone was not the place to be out in the open in a thunder storm. Everyone now knew that their lives were in great danger.

Collapse

Eventually, with great difficulty, Krakauer made it back to the South Col camp at around 7 p.m. His oxygen had run out long before. He collapsed in his tent, totally and utterly exhausted. He was one of the lucky ones. Above him, desperate people were fighting for their lives against the anger of the blizzard that had developed.

EXTREME FACTS
BLIZZARDS

A blizzard is caused when a strong wind whips up falling snow or snow lying on the ground. Blizzards can be extremely dangerous. It is very difficult to see or hear anything in them because the snow blocks up your eyes and ears. You hear a terrible roaring in your ears and all you can see is a whirling whiteness. It is easy to get lost even just outside your tent. Climbers have walked off the side of Everest into the sheer drops below during bad blizzards.

Huddled together

Later that evening, a group of climbers managed to get back to within fifteen minutes' walk from the South Col camp. Krakauer and the others who had returned earlier had no idea of this as they listened to the winds battering their tents, worrying that they would be blown away.

Now, near by, in the wild storm, eleven people huddled together behind a rock that was hardly bigger than a washing-machine. They had struggled with great difficulty down the side of the mountain. Although they were now on the South Col, the blizzard was so fierce they could not make out the camp's tents. It was difficult even to stand up, especially as they were drained from long hours of climbing. None had any bottled oxygen left.

If they set off in the wrong direction they could fall off the edge to certain death thousands of metres below. The two guides with them, Groom and Beidleman, prayed that the strong wind would drop in time for them to go and look for the tents — 'in time' meaning before they all lost consciousness. The wind-chill factor was an incredible −73°C.

EXTREME FACTS
WIND CHILL

The wind can make the temperature of the air feel much colder than it really is. This is called the wind-chill factor. Usually, a thin layer of warm air surrounds your body, but if the wind is strong, this layer of warm air is blown away and you feel colder. A gentle breeze can make you feel about 3°C cooler. In a strong breeze the drop might be 10°C. In the fierce winds on the high slopes of Everest, the drop in temperature is much, much greater and extremely dangerous.

Just before midnight the sky cleared a little and they could see a few stars. Though the wind was still roaring from the direction in which they had to go, six of the stranded climbers managed to struggle their way to the tents. It took them about forty-five minutes. Then another guide from the camp, Anatoli Boukreev, tried to return to the spot to collect the five remaining.

Due to his bravery and determination (he risked his life each time he went back into the blizzard), by dawn all but two had been helped back. They had been left because they were believed to be on the point of death. The other climbers were so close to death themselves that it was felt better to save what little energy they had to help themselves and those who were likely to live.

How can anyone be asked to choose what to do in this kind of situation? Do you try to save someone who is in a very bad way and is probably unlikely to live, if it could mean the death of everyone else in the group who has a chance of living? Life-and-death decisions on Everest are very difficult.

Higher up

Even higher on the mountain, others had been caught by the terrible storm. The leader of Adventure Consultants, Rob Hall, a very experienced climber, had been trapped at the top of the Hillary Step, trying to help a client. He made it to the South Summit but didn't have the energy to go lower. Two Sherpas tried to get up to him the next day but the winds were too strong and they had to turn back 200 m below him. Hall had a radio attached to his jacket lapel and from the top of this lonely mountain the Base Camp Manager linked him up via satellite telephone to his pregnant wife in New Zealand. His wife tried to encourage him, but she herself had climbed Everest and knew that his situation was really impossible. She knew it was unlikely she would ever see him again.

Other climbers found his body in a small protected snow-ledge by the South Summit a few days later. The client, Doug Hanson, whom he had been helping, was nowhere to be seen. Nor was there any sign of the other guide, Andy Harris, who is believed to have been with them.

A little way further down the mountain, on the South-East Ridge, the leader of Mountain Madness, Scott Fischer, had also been struggling for his life in the storm. Tragically, he lost the fight as well. Fischer and Hall had both been very skilful and experienced mountaineers. The mountain had claimed climbers of all abilities in that awful weather.

Still alive

But what seemed like a miracle occurred among all the tragedies. American Beck Weathers, left for dead on the South Col, regained consciousness and managed, somehow, to stagger back to the camp. The others were amazed. They could not believe he had survived. They rushed him to a spare tent and put him on oxygen. Weathers' face and hands were severely frostbitten, but he hung on to life.

Eventually, with help, he and the others descended to just above the Khumbu Ice-fall. Weathers was airlifted out by helicopter, together with a Taiwanese climber who also had terrible frostbite. Neither of them would have been able to make their way down the ice-fall and it would have been impossible for the others to have carried them over the rickety ladder-bridges across the many crevasses.

Once away from Everest, Weathers had to have a great deal of surgery. His right arm was amputated halfway below his elbow, as well as all the fingers and thumb on his left hand. His nose was removed and remade with tissue from his ear and forehead.

But he did have his life.

A terrible tragedy
The number of deaths in this violent storm in May 1996 made it one of the worst tragedies on Everest since seven porters were killed in 1924 (see page 37). No one can guarantee success on the highest mountain in the world. Luck – good and bad always plays a part in everyone's attempt on the summit. Ever since people started trying to climb Everest disasters have occurred – and they will continue to happen, even with the most modern twenty-first-century equipment and communications.

EVEREST TODAY

In the twenty-first century Everest is still a great draw for people. Expeditions of all kinds come to the mountain. These include experienced mountaineers trying to climb new and dangerous routes, as well as paying clients who just want the 'easiest' route to the top. There can be as many as 600 people at the Nepalese Base Camp in April!

As you can see from the table opposite, a lot of money is charged for visas (permission to enter the country) and permits (permission to climb Everest). Both Nepal and Tibet are poor countries and this money adds greatly to the income of each.

Apart from the paperwork, the costs of putting together an Everest expedition are very high, which is why many expeditions try to attract sponsors. These costs will vary, depending on each expedition and individual climbers' needs. For example, if you have your own guide, this will add greatly to the costs.

Some costs for an Everest climber

	£
Permits (for team)	45,000
Flights and visas (per person)	600
Oxygen cylinders (for team)	50,000
Climbing equipment (per person)	2,000
Tents and sleeping-bags (per person)	2,800

Other costs

Yak and porters	5,000
Sherpas	2,000 each
Laptop (so you can have a web site at Base Camp) and camera	1,500

GETTING THERE

Nowadays most climbers fly to Kathmandu in Nepal and then spend three weeks trekking the 160 km to Everest Base Camp. This walk is part of their acclimatization programme, with the route varying from 1,500 m to over 5,000 m. Then they spend a further month acclimatizing to higher altitudes by climbing up to the lower camps on the slopes of Everest before they aim to be taken to the summit by guides early in May.

Trekking

But not all visitors to the slopes of Everest are there to climb it. Many are trekkers who want to walk through the Himalayas to Base Camp. Often they are linked to a particular expedition (e.g. the Irish expedition in 1993 had three trekking groups who visited them). These trekkers help contribute towards the costs of the expedition and also help raise sponsorship and awareness at home. They can feel they are very much part of the expedition and join in with the excitement of the preparations and organization of the summit team.

The make-up of an Everest summit team

Actually there is no typical Everest summit team! The following is just to give you an idea:

Climbers	8
Climbing Sherpas	0–8

(commercial expeditions take more climbing Sherpas to give their clients as much chance as possible of reaching the top)

Base Camp manager	1
Team doctor (at Base Camp)	1

Sherpa assistants and cooks   as many as
                                               the expedition
                                               can afford!

Commercial expeditions also have one or more
guides, depending on what the clients are prepared to
pay for.

ENVIRONMENT

All these visitors to Everest obviously have the potential to
harm the mountain environment. Early climbers didn't think
of taking their rubbish and old equipment away with them
because the mountain was so big and there were few
visitors. But, by the 1980s, as more people came to it,
the slopes began to get very cluttered. In some of the higher
parts there were hundreds of empty oxygen bottles
everywhere.

The international governing body for mountaineers got
together to discuss this. The result was the Kathmandu
Declaration, which gives guidelines for people climbing
Everest. For example, they are advised to remove their
rubbish from the slopes. Climbers are also asked to respect
the local culture and customs of the area. Some expeditions
have been especially organized with the aim of clearing up
the mountain. Tibet and Nepal have also set their own
environmental rules for climbers.

Nowadays the very fact that such large numbers of
people are on the mountain means that everyone must be
more aware of clearing up behind them, though some
expeditions are better at this than others. Sherpas are also
now paid an extra sum of money for any rubbish and each
empty oxygen bottle they bring down.

Conditions are not as bad as they were in the 1980s, but climbers must continue to be careful otherwise the mountain will be spoilt for all.

EVEREST — THE FUTURE

So what does the future hold for Everest? There are those who feel that too many people now go to Everest. Should some people be stopped from climbing Everest? Should guided expeditions be allowed?

The critics think that the type of people who attempt to climb the mountain should be limited. There have been debates on whether only climbers without bottled oxygen should be allowed to attempt the summit. This would put off many of the less able climbers. But, so far, the only limit comes from the number of permits that Nepal and Tibet issue each year.

What do you think? Should people be prevented from trying to attempt their greatest ambition, even if it is so dangerous? Is it good that so many people can now try to reach the summit of Everest?

Perhaps you are already a keen mountaineer, perhaps Everest is on the list of mountains you wish to climb. Or perhaps you might want to trek to Everest Base Camp one day.

If you do get there, remember to respect the height, altitude, weather and environment of this amazing part of our planet. Remember, too, its thrilling climbing history.

EVEREST TIMELINE

800s	According to legend, a Buddhist monk was carried to the top of Everest on a ray of sunlight.
1854	Declared the highest mountain in the world by British army map-makers and marked on their maps as 'Peak XV'.
1865	Named 'Everest' after Sir George Everest.
1921	First British expedition (from Tibet). Climbers reach the North Col.
1922	Second British expedition (from Tibet). Climbers reach 8,320 m.
1924	Third British expedition (from Tibet). Mallory and Irvine disappear. Somervell and Norton reach 8,578 m without bottled oxygen.
1930s	Four official British expeditions.

1934	Maurice Wilson, 'the Mad Yorkshireman', makes an unofficial attempt to climb Everest. Although he has little experience of climbing or piloting, he flies his Gypsy Moth aeroplane, 'Ever-Wrest', from England to India, and makes his way to the mountain to try and climb it solo. His body is found the following year in a glacier.
1951	The first British expedition to approach Everest from the Nepalese side. Led by Eric Shipton. Climbers (including Edmund Hillary) cross the Khumbu Ice-fall and reach the entrance to the Western Cwm.
1952	A Swiss expedition (including Sherpa Tenzing Norgay) nearly reaches the South Summit.
1953	A British expedition led by John Hunt. On 29 May 1953, Edmund Hillary (New Zealander) and Sherpa Tenzing Norgay (Indian) reach the summit itself via the South-East Ridge.
1956	A Swiss expedition reaches the summit.

Since the 1950s there have been many other expeditions to climb Everest. Here are just some of the key ones:

1960	A Chinese expedition reaches the summit by the North and North-East ridges (i.e., from Tibet). Summit team members are Wang Fu Chou and Chu Yin Hua, and Tibetan climber Gonbu.
1963	Americans Tom Hornbein and Willi Unsoeld are the first to climb up by one route and descend by another – up

by the West Ridge and down by the South-East Ridge. They are also the first to climb the West Ridge.

1975   Junko Tabei, from Japan, becomes the first woman to summit Everest on 16 May. She climbs via the South Col and the South-East Ridge. Eleven days later, on 27 May, Tibetan climber, Phantog, becomes the second woman to the top. She climbs via the North and the North-East Ridge.

1975   A British team (expedition leader Sir Chris Bonington) summits Everest via the South-West Face – Dougal Haston, Doug Scott, Peter Boardman, Sherpa Pertemba and Mick Burke reach the top. Burke tragically disappears on summit day, but he is believed to have reached the top.

1978   Reinhold Messner (Italian) and Peter Habeler (Austrian) are the first people to reach the top of Everest without bottled oxygen.

1980   First winter ascent of Everest, 17 February, by two Polish climbers, Leszek Cichy and Krzysztof Wielicki.

1980   Reinhold Messner makes the first solo climb of Everest without bottled oxygen.

1983   An American expedition reaches the summit by the East (Kangshung) Face.

1984   An Australian expedition reaches the summit via the Great (Norton) Couloir on the North Face. The summiting team is Tim Macartney-Snape and Greg Mortimer.

1988	An international team (including Steve Venables, British) sets up a new route on the East Face. Venables summits alone – the first British climber to do so without bottled oxygen
1988	Frenchman Jean-Marc Boivin carries a parapente (a light, steerable parachute) to the summit and jumps off! The parapente opens above him and he takes eleven minutes to descend 2,440 m to the Western Cwm.
1993	Rebecca Stephens is the first British woman to summit Everest.
1995	British climber Alison Hargreaves is the first woman ever to reach the summit of Everest alone without bottled oxygen.
1996	A very bad storm on the South Col route claims the lives of five people (including two guides) on commercial expeditions on 10–12 May.
1998	Tom Whittaker is the first disabled climber to reach the summit. (He had lost a foot in a car accident nineteen years before.)
2000	Davo Karnicar, from Slovenia, successfully skis from the top of Everest to Base Camp at 5,300 m in five hours.

IMPORTANT EVEREST LANDMARKS

Summit	8,848 m
South Summit	8,763 m
Second Step	8,595 m
First Step	8,498 m
South Col	7,986 m
West Shoulder	7,254 m
North Col	7,010 m
Western Cwm	6,157 m
Khumbu Ice-fall	5,486 m

GLOSSARY

Abseiling
When a climber uses a rope to go down a steep drop in a controlled way. The rope is fixed at the top. Nowadays the climber is usually attached to it by a form of clip that works as a brake if they should slip.

Acclimatize
To become accustomed to a new climate or to new conditions. Mountaineers need to climb very high mountains in gradual stages in order to slowly become acclimatized to the difficulty of breathing oxygen in the thin air.

Airlift
To be transported away by aircraft, usually in an emergency.

Alpine Club
An organization founded by climbers in England in 1857, when British climbers in the Alps were making many first ascents. It still exists and members climb difficult mountains all over the world.

Altitude
The height of something in relation to sea level or ground level. At high altitudes, in places like mountain peaks, it can be hard to breathe properly because it is more difficult for the body to obtain

oxygen from the air. This may cause an illness called altitude sickness.

Altitude sickness
An illness caused by climbing to a high altitude. The shortage of oxygen can make you feel sick, exhausted and cause you to hyperventilate (breathe very fast).

Ascent
A climb or walk to the summit of a mountain or hill (see Descent).

Avalanche
A mass of snow, sometimes with ice and rocks, falling rapidly down a mountainside.

Base Camp
A camp made fairly low down on a mountain. Expeditions to higher parts of the mountain are organized from this point.

Belay
To fix a running rope round an object such as a rock. Climbers work together, with one climber (the belayer) managing the rope while the other climbs. If the climber slips, the belayer tries to stop the fall by using the secured running rope, which is also anchored around the belayer's body.

Bivouac
A bivouac is a temporary camp, usually made overnight. In an emergency bivouac, there may not be tents or cover and the person must try to get shelter in any way possible, e.g., digging a hole in the snow.

Blizzard
A severe snowstorm with high winds.

Bull beef
Beef that has been preserved (in salt water) and tinned to stop it going off. It is also called bully beef or corned beef.

Calorie
A unit of heat energy. It is usually used to measure the energy contained in food. Most adults need 2,000–3,000 calories a day in order to live.

Col
The lowest point of a ridge between two peaks, a col usually forms a pass from one side of a mountain range to another.

Cornice
An overhanging ledge of snow, often looking a bit like the crest of a wave. The high winds that whip around mountains form the snow into peaks that overhang the firmer snow, ice and rock below. Cornices are very dangerous to climb.

Couloir
A channel or gully on a mountain. Couloirs can be filled with ice, snow or rubble. They are natural routes for avalanches and so need to be treated with caution, especially in warm weather or during the day when the risk is highest. Therefore, couloirs are usually climbed at night with a head-torch when the ground is frozen.

Crampon
A metal plate with spikes fixed to a boot for walking on ice or rock climbing.

Crevasse
A deep, open crack, often found in glaciers.

Cwm
This is a Welsh word (pronounced 'coom') meaning an area ringed by mountains. The Western Cwm was named by George Mallory in the 1920s.

The Death Zone
The Death Zone is the name that mountaineers have given to the upper part of Everest – above 8,000 m. Because there is so little oxygen available here, climbers' bodies begin to get weaker and weaker. If they stay too long at this altitude they will

eventually die. That is why, when climbers reach this height, they must get to the summit within a day or two or go down to a lower camp.

Degree
A degree is a unit of measurement. There are two different kinds of degrees. One type is used for measuring angles and slopes, the other type is used to measure temperature in Celsius or Fahrenheit.

Dehydration
To lose a large amount of water from the body. Mountaineers on Everest lose water by sweating and by breathing hard in the cold dry air. They need a lot of liquid in order to avoid becoming seriously dehydrated.

Descent
When climbers come down mountains, they make their descent (see Ascent).

Detour
A long or roundabout route that is taken to avoid something or perhaps to make a visit along the way.

Exposure
When the body is exposed to very cold temperatures and bad weather conditions. Exposure is a serious condition that can affect stranded climbers or those caught in snowstorms.

Face
A vertical or sloping side of a mountain.

Frostbite
A condition common in very cold climates, when body tissue becomes so cold that it freezes. This can result in gangrene (when the flesh dies) and the climber may lose toes, fingers and even limbs. In very serious cases, the person may die.

Glacier
A huge mass of snow and ice which moves slowly under its own weight.

Glare

A strong or dazzling light. Glare can be especially strong in high mountains due to the reflection of sunlight on the snow (see Snow-blindness).

Hypothermia

A very dangerous condition that happens when the body loses heat and its temperature falls below 35°C. This is usually caused by being outside in very cold conditions without enough protection (see Exposure).

Ice-fall

A steep part of a glacier, like a frozen waterfall. Ice-falls can be very dangerous because huge towers of ice can suddenly fall and crush mountaineers.

Jetstream

The fast, strong currents of the high-level winds that circle the earth between 8.8–12.8 km, above sea-level.

Lethargy

A lack of energy and enthusiasm, which can have many causes. For mountaineers it is often a side-effect of acclimatization. It is also one of the symptoms of hypothermia.

Monsoon

The name of a wind which blows in from the Arabian Sea over India to the Himalayas from June to September.

Mule

A mule is a cross between a donkey and a horse, and is often used for carrying heavy loads.

Nausea

A feeling of sickness, often followed by vomiting.

Oxygen

Air is made up of different gases, including oxygen. At high altitudes our bodies find it difficult to breathe in enough oxygen, so many mountaineers carry bottles of this gas to help them breathe more easily and continue climbing to higher parts.

Peak
The pointed top of a mountain.

Pemmican
Dried beef and beef fat, moulded into blocks. This was often eaten on early expeditions because it was easy to carry and nutritious.

Permit
A permit is a card of permission that must be obtained and paid for before entering certain places. Mountaineers need to have a permit in order to climb Everest.

Plateau
An area of high, level ground.

Porter
A person employed to carry loads. On expeditions local porters often accompany the climbers.

Puja
A religious prayer ceremony carried out by the peoples of the Himalayas to ask the mountain gods for protection and for permission to climb a holy mountain like Everest.

Reconnaissance
Sometimes shortened to 'recce', this is preliminary research or surveying, usually made before a difficult climb or expedition.

Ridge
A long, narrow strip of land with sloping sides formed where two mountain faces meet.

Royal Geographical Society (RGS)
A society founded in London in 1830 for 'the advancement of

geographical science'. The organization still exists today.

SAS
Initials of the Special Air Service. A specialist army regiment trained in commando techniques of warfare.

Sherpa
Sherpa is the name of a group of people from the Nepalese side of Everest, in and around the Khumbu region. Because they have been born and live in the high Himalayas, they are used to working in the thin air here. These people work as porters and assistants for expeditions climbing Everest. The Sherpas are famous for their climbing skills, their strength and their ability to work at high altitudes. Nowadays the term Sherpa is often used to refer to anyone from the Himalayas who works as a porter.

Sirdar
The head of the Sherpas on an expedition is called the Sirdar.

Snow-blindness
A very painful eye condition caused by the bright glare of the snow and ice. Snow goggles should be worn to prevent this.

Sponsor
A person or organization that provides funds for a project or activity often in return for advertising and publicity.

Squall (snow squall)
A sudden, violent storm.

Summit
The highest point of a hill or mountain.

Surveyor
A person who examines and records the features of an area of land in order to make a map, plan or description.

Traversing
To go across the side of a mountain diagonally or horizontally,

often because obstructions make it impossible to go upwards, or because the ridge is not suitable to walk along.

Trek
To go on a long journey on foot. Mountaineers usually trek for many days to get to Everest, which helps them acclimatize.

Ultra-violet light (UV)
An important component of sunlight. However, too much exposure can be harmful to the eyes and skin. On Everest, the thin air means that the UV light is stronger than in lower places and special glasses giving 100 per cent protection are needed.

Veteran
A person who has had long experience in a particular field.

Wind-chill factor
In very cold climates, the strength of the wind can have a great effect on your body temperature, making you even colder. This is the wind-chill factor.

Yak
A large, domesticated wild ox used in Tibet as a pack animal and for its milk, meat and hide.

FURTHER
EXPLORATION

If you would like to find out more about the people and the expeditions described in this book, or about mountaineering in general, there are many things you can do. Look out for exhibitions and events at museums and libraries. Mountaineers often give slide shows and talks when they return from an expedition. Your local library and newspaper will probably have details of these. You can also ask your librarian for books about Everest and climbing. There are various websites on the Internet you can explore, too.

Places to visit and things to do

Exhibitions on Everest and mountaineering in general at the National Museum of Mountaineering, Rheged Centre, Cumbria.

Major Bronco Lane's frostbitten fingers which he lost on an Everest expedition are at the National Army Museum, Chelsea, London.

If you would like to go with an adult to try an indoor climbing wall, check the British Mountaineering Council (BMC) website (see below) for details of the one nearest you. The BMC also runs programmes for young members, called 'Gripped'. Find out details via their web site below or contact them at 117–179 Burton Road, Manchester M20 2BB.

Web sites to visit
The British Mountaineering Council: http://www.thebmc.co.uk
For information on your nearest indoor climbing wall:
http://www.thebmc.co.uk/indoor/walls/wall.asp
For information on the BMC's schemes for young members:
http://www.thebmc.co.uk/gripped/h.m
For general information on Everest and Everest expeditions:
http://www.mnteverest.com
http://www.everestnews.com
http://www.classic.mountainzone.com/climbing

Some books on Everest you might enjoy reading
Davidson, Bob, *Mallory and Tenzing Climb Everest*, Zoë Borks Ltd, UK, 1993
Gillman, Peter (editor), *Everest: The Best Writing & Pictures from Over Seventy Years of Human Endeavour*, Little, Brown & Co., London, 1993
Hemmleb, Jochen, Johnson, Larry A., and Simonson, Eric R., *Ghosts of Everest*, Macmillan, London, 1999
Jenkins, Steve, *The Top of the World*, Houghton Mifflin, Boston, 1999
Tibballs, Geoff, *Everest: The Struggle to Reach the Top of the World*, Carlton, 1998

Films about Everest
Everest is a large-screen IMAX film made by David Breashears in 1996. Look out for it if you have an IMAX cinema near you.
Various videos have been made about expeditions to Everest.
See if your local library has one.

Bibliography
Anker, Conrad, and Roberts, David, *The Lost Explorer: Finding*

Mallory on Mount Everest, Robinson, London, 1999

Ball, Steve (editor), *Seven Summits*, Mitchell Beazley, London, 2000

Birkett, Bill, and Peascod, Bill, *Women Climbing: 200 Years of Achievement*, A. N. C. Blackman, 1989

Bonington, Chris (editor), *Great Climbs*, Mitchell Beazley, London, 1995

Bonington, Chris, *Everest, The Hard Way*, Hodder, London, 1976

Breashears, David, and Salkeld, Audrey, *The Last Climb*, National Geographic Society, Washington, DC, 1999

Breashears, David, *High Exposure*, Canongate, Edinburgh, 1999

Child, Greg, *Climbing: The Complete Reference*, Facts on File Inc., New York, 1995

Coburn, Broughton, *Everest: Mountain without Mercy*, National Geographic Society, Washington, DC, 1997

Davidson, Bob, *Mallory and Tenzing Climb Everest*, Zoë Borks Ltd, UK, 1993

Douglas, Ed, *Chomolungma Sings the Blues: Travels Round Everest*, 1997

Finlay, Hugh, Everist, Richard, Wheeler, Tony, *Nepal*, Lonely Planet, London, 1997

Gillman, Peter (editor), *Everest: The Best Writing & Pictures from over Seventy Years of Human Endeavour*, Little, Brown & Co., London, 1993

Hattington, Garth, *The Climbers' Handbook*.

Hemmleb, Jochen, Johnson, Larry A., & Simonson, Eric R., *Ghosts of Everest*, Macmillan, London, 1999

Holzel, Tom, and Salkeld, Audrey, *The Mystery of Mallory & Irvine*, Pimlico, London, 1999

Hunt, John, *The Ascent of Everest*, Hodder & Stoughton, Kent, 1993

Jenkins, Steve, *The Top of the World*, Houghton Mifflin, Boston, 1999

Krakauer, Jon, *Into Thin Air*, Pan Books, London, 1998

Messner, Reinhold, *Everest: Expedition to the Ultimate*, The
Mountaineers' Books, England, 1999

Messner, Reinhold, *My Quest for the Yeti: Confronting the
Himalayas' Deepest Mystery*, Macmillan, London, 2000

Rose, David, and Douglas, Ed, *Regions of the Heart (The
Triumph & Tragedy of Alison Hargreaves)*, Michael Joseph,
1999

Salkeld, Audrey (general editor), *World Mountaineering*,
Mitchell Beazley, London, 1998

Siggins, Lorna, *Everest Calling*, Mainstream Publishing,
Edinburgh, 1994

Tibballs, Geoff, *Everest: The Struggle to Reach the Top of the
World*, Carlton, 1998

Unsworth, Walt, *Everest: The Mountaineering History*, Barton
Wicks Publications, London, 2000

Venables, Stephen, *Everest: Alone at the Summit*, Odyssey
Books, Bath, 1996

Willis, Clint, *High: Stories of Survival from Everest and K2*,
Adrenaline, New York, 1999

**The author would like to thank the following organ-
izations for their assistance:**
Royal Geographical Society, London
Expedition Advisory Centre, RGS, London
The Alpine Club, London
The British Mountaineering Council, Manchester
Libraries in Belfast and County Down, Northern Ireland

The author would also like to thank Dawson Stelfox, Margaret
Ecclestone, Shane Winser, Anna McCormack, Brett Hannam,
Lesley Crymble, Robin Charley, Jo Hopkins, Mary Crowe, P. J.
Gault, Karl Partridge and all the other individuals who have
helped her with this book and her other expedition books. She
would particularly like to thank her editor, Amanda Li.

INDEX

Numbers in bold type refer to illustrations or to pages where the word is defined

Acknowledgements

The author and publishers would like to thank the following for permission to include copyrighted quotations in this book:

Page 2 Quotation by Tenzing Norgay from *Man of Everest* by James Ramsey Ullman, reprinted with permission of Chambers Harrap Publishers Ltd. *Man of Everest* was first published by George G Harrap.

Page 2 Quotation by Reinhold Messner from *To the Top of the World* by Reinhold Messner, published by the Crowood Press Ltd, The Stable Block, Crowood Lane, Ramsbury, Malborough, SN8 2HR, e-mail: enquiries@crowood.com. Tel: 01672 520320.

Page 3 Quotation by Chris Bonington, reprinted with kind permission of Sir Chris Bonington, CBE.

Page 3 Quotation by Dawson Stelfox, from *Everest Calling* by Lorna Siggins, Mainstream Publishing, Edinburgh, Scotland.

Page 31 Quotation by E F Norton from *The Fight for Everest*, Edward Arnold.

Page 49 Quotation by Conrad Anker from *Ghosts of Everest* by Jochen Hemmleb, Larry A Johnson and Eric R Simonson, Macmillan Publishers Ltd, London, 1999.

Pages 72, 73, 74 Quotations by Sir Edmund Hillary from *The Ascent of Everest* by John Hunt, reproduced by permission of Hodder and Stoughton Ltd.

Page 85 Quotation by Chris Bonington, reprinted with kind permission of Sir Chris Bonington, CBE.

Page 92 Quotation by Reinhold Messner, reprinted with kind permission of Reinhold Messner.

Photography Credits

Photograph, page 1 © John Cleare/Mountain Camera
Photograph, page 8 © John Cleare/Mountain Camera
Photograph, page 10 © John Cleare/Mountain Camera
Photograph, page 54 supplied by Mary Evans Picture Library
Photograph, page 60 © John Cleare/Mountain Camera
Photograph, page 64 © John Cleare/Mountain Camera
Photograph, page 75 © Sir Edmund Hillary, supplied by RGS Picture Library
Photograph, page 80 © Doug Scott/Mountain Camera
Photograph, page 87 © Colin Monteath/Mountain Camera
Photograph, page 99 © Doug Scott/Mountain Camera